The Sky is no Longer the Limit

The Sky is no Longer the Limit

A flight plan to success for immigrants with big dreams

SVETLANA LAZAREVA

Copyright © 2015 Svetlana Lazareva
All rights reserved. All Rights Reserved. No part of this book may be used or reproduced by any means, graphic, electronic, or mechanical, including photocopying, recording, taping or by any information storage retrieval system without written permission of the author except for brief quotations in articles and reviews.

Editors: Anne Toner Fung and Bonnie Gross
Translator and Editor: Karl Marx
Photographer: Elena Dolgy
Cover design and illustrations: Dmitry Zhukovsky

ISBN-13: 9780994861207
ISBN-10: 0994861206

ImmPress Institute *ImmPressInstitute.com*

To my husband, Denis, and my two sons, Danila and Vlado Ivan: three men who have brought happiness and true meaning into my life.

"The greater danger for most of us lies
not in setting our aim too high and falling short;
but in setting our aim too low, and achieving our mark".

Michelangelo

Acknowledgements

It takes many people to create anything. So many of you invested your time in me and in this book, and I want to take this opportunity to thank you all.

Relatives – I love you all. Thank you for keeping my heart in place, for your love, confidence, friendship and inspiration.

Extremely talented friends and professionals - thank you for your contributions to different areas of creating the book. Thank you for believing in me, for your encouragement and for keeping my spirits high.

Toastmasters – thank you for helping me find my voice and for your incredible listening and support.

Toronto Public Transportation and Go Transit – thank you for providing a comfortable place where most of my book was written.

Challenges – to all the situations and people who made the journey difficult - thank you for making me rise to each occasion and experience my true power.

And finally, myself - for staying strong and keeping my eyes on fulfilling this dream.

Table of Contents

Preamble · xv
Introduction · xvii

OUTSIDE, LOOKING IN 1
Chapter 1   Discover Why You are in Canada · · · · · · · · · · ·3
Chapter 2   Burn Your Bridges· · · · · · · · · · · · · · · · · · ·5
Chapter 3   Define Success ·7
Chapter 4   Claim Your Right to be Happy · · · · · · · · · · ·10
Chapter 5   Take Care · 14
Chapter 6   Be Regret Free · 17
Chapter 7   Find Yourself · 21
Chapter 8   Who Makes Your Choices? · · · · · · · · · · · · · 25
Chapter 9   Make Your Own News · · · · · · · · · · · · · · · 27

INSIDE, LOOKING OUT 31
Chapter 10 What Do You Think of Me? · · · · · · · · · · · · 33
Chapter 11 Be Open to Opportunities · · · · · · · · · · · · · 35
Chapter 12 The Power of No · · · · · · · · · · · · · · · · · · · 39
Chapter 13 Be Optimistic · 42
Chapter 14 Serve and Get Fulfilled · · · · · · · · · · · · · · · 45
Chapter 15 Bite Off as Much as You Can Chew · · · · · · · · 48
Chapter 16 What is Your Money Psychology? · · · · · · · · · 56

THE VIEW FROM HERE 63
Chapter 17 RESP, RRSP and More · · · · · · · · · · · · · · · · · ·65
Chapter 18 Have Peace of Mind ·71
Chapter 19 Life is…. ·74
Chapter 20 You are What You Eat · · · · · · · · · · · · · · · · · · 76
Chapter 21 Music and Laughter · · · · · · · · · · · · · · · · · · · 80
Chapter 22 Happy Parents - Happy Kids · · · · · · · · · · · · ·82
Chapter 23 Stick or Split · 88
Chapter 24 Workplace Culture ·91
Chapter 25 Small Talk is Big Talk · · · · · · · · · · · · · · · · · · ·93

JUST DO IT 97
Chapter 26 Have a Plan · 99
Chapter 27 Work on Your Plan ·103
Chapter 28 Develop Good Habits · · · · · · · · · · · · · · · · ·106
Chapter 29 The Power of Asking · · · · · · · · · · · · · · · · · · 108
Chapter 30 Choose your Employer · · · · · · · · · · · · · · · · 112
Chapter 31 Market Yourself · 115
Chapter 32 Educate Yourself · 118
Chapter 33 Do You Speak English? · · · · · · · · · · · · · · · ·120
Chapter 34 Know Your Rights ·122
Chapter 35 Find a Mentor · 125
Chapter 36 Explore and Feel at Home · · · · · · · · · · · · · 127
Chapter 37 You are Unique · 129
Chapter 38 Write the Next Chapter of This Book · · · · · · · · · · · ·130

Preamble

Toronto, Pearson International Airport.
An unusually warm Canadian winter?
People in shorts and straw hats pass by. Their souls are still filled with the ocean, champagne sparkles and joy. So many tanned happy Canadians, sure of their day today and tomorrow, coming back to their family hearths after sunny vacations.

Two newcomers, clad in sheepskin coats, fur caps with flaps over their ears, sweating, waiting in the immigration line. Two suitcases each, containing all the belongings they brought with them. No friends, no relatives: just the two of them in a New Land. They had no English (or French) and little money. They were two people against a whole world. They were alone, lost, and scared. But they were hungry for life, for a better life.

Seven years later…
There are four of them now. The family has grown by two boys. They know hundreds of people. Many of them are friends. They speak English well. They make enough money to live comfortably in a big house and drive good cars.

Now they call Canada Home.
How did they do it?
They did not know the secret then. They just followed their instincts for what was right; taking one step each day, no matter what. They were always moving towards their dream - to make Canada home, the best place to be.

Introduction

Canada is populated by people who once upon a time arrived here from somewhere else. First Nations people are the only ones who belonged in Canada from the beginning. We all came after. Some of us came 200 years ago, some came last month and some will come tomorrow.

All of us came to Canada with expectations and dreams. How many of us made our dreams come true? How many of us remember that we had a dream?

It is never too late to follow that dream.

This book is dedicated to you. It holds the key to Success. It holds the key to Your_success. The question is: will you see it, will you grab hold of it and will you use it?

No matter when you came to Canada.
　　No matter how good your English (or French) is.
　　No matter how old you are.
　　No matter where you came from.

What matters is...where you are going!

Do you want to change your life?
　　Are you willing to challenge yourself...and change?

The secret to success exists. However, knowing the secret is not enough to reach success. You need to be ready to work hard and do whatever it takes to reach your goal. And I will be there to help you every step of the way.

You can blame everything that stands between you and success.
    You can spend the rest of your life finding excuses.
    The key is this: if you do not change what you do and how you do it, nothing else will change.

To support your journey through this book and make it more memorable, I have provided space to write notes, jot down ideas and make plans.

Dream big and you too can have everything you want and deserve.

Seven years ago I could not speak English. I thought I would never be able to learn the language. I could not even pronounce "thank you" so that people would understand me.
    Seven years ago I had no job. I was sending hundreds of résumés out without a single response.
    Now I have written this book to share my journey and to inspire you. I was lost and scared just like you and now I am strong.

The sky is no longer the limit for me.
If I could do it, so can you!

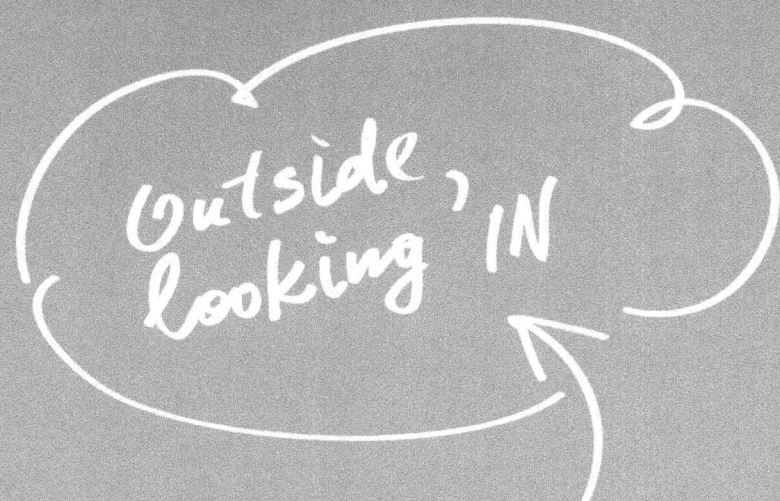

Outside, looking IN

Before you can achieve anything,
you need to know yourself. Start your journey
to success and happiness
by looking inward.

"Knowing yourself is the beginning
of all wisdom".
Aristotle

Chapter 1

Discover Why You are in Canada

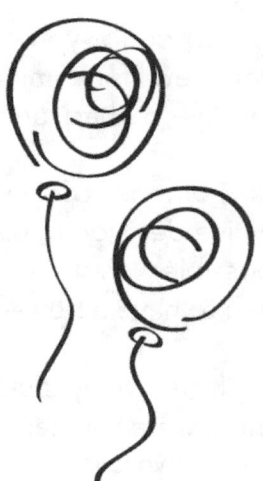

You may have been born in Canada, you may have been brought here as a child, or you may be the one who made a conscious decision to come to Canada.

If you are an immigrant, a pioneer, then remind yourself why you first decided to come to Canada.

What made you leave your homeland, family, friends, job and comfort zone to come here?

What motivated you to make one of the most important decisions of your life?

Remind yourself and take credit for coming here. Clearly you have a great base to build on as you move towards success. You have the decisiveness, strength, courage and willpower that brought you far from home to this new place.

No doubt you came here for a better life. Visualize yourself in your new life. Remind yourself how you felt coming here, the expectations you had, and what you dreamt of.

For those of you who were brought to Canada and were not the active decision maker, go to the person who made that decision (if possible), and ask questions. Don't accept the answer "I wanted you to have a better life here". Ask exactly what they mean by that.

I met many students during my first years in Canada. Most of them were not happy about leaving their friends, their schools and their towns. They were angry. They didn't want to come to Canada in the first place; now they had to adjust to a new country and survive in a new school.

Ask questions and try to understand what motivated your family. If you are still angry, forgive them. You cannot move on and be successful if you are angry. This anger is holding you back – so let it go. You cannot change your past but you can form your future – and only you can decide what it will look like.

If you belong to the group who were born here, you have some homework to do too.
Learn why your ancestors came here. Learn about your roots. Talk to your relatives. Look up the history of immigration to Canada and discover the "who, why, when and how" behind your presence here.

Everything happens for a reason. If you are here, it was meant to be. Thank your ancestors for bringing you here. Some of you may want to go back to your country of origin and try to be successful there. But I can save you a trip by telling you that Canada is the best place to be. And if you cannot (read "do not want to") be successful here, you likely will not be successful anywhere else. Your success is determined by you alone, not by the place you live.

Chapter 2

Burn Your Bridges

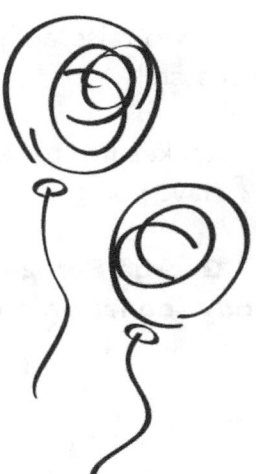

The expression to "burn bridges" comes from the history of military campaigns, when commanders ordered their men to burn bridges after defeating an army, saving the soldiers the temptation of retreat.

I have met newcomers to Canada who came to "try to live" here. Some took vacation from work for three or four weeks to come and look around; some kept their business or a job back home. By doing these things, you set yourself up for failure. I am not suggesting selling all your belongings and assets before coming to Canada. However, simply "testing the waters" indicates that you have a fall-back plan, just in case you are not successful here.

Can you feel the difference between the phrases: "IF I become successful" and "WHEN I become successful"? Using the word IF means you are keeping a connecting thread between you and the country you came from. When you say "IF", you are setting yourself up for disappointment.

Burn your bridges and don't look back. Grant yourself the time to establish yourself in your new land. Give yourself enough time to realize your success. Everything takes time. It takes time to grow a tree, to raise a child, to build a house. It takes time to become successful.

It takes five to seven years to be good at something.
Have you given yourself that much time?

George Bernard Shaw said: "Everything happens to everybody sooner or later if there is time enough".

Chapter 3

DEFINE SUCCESS

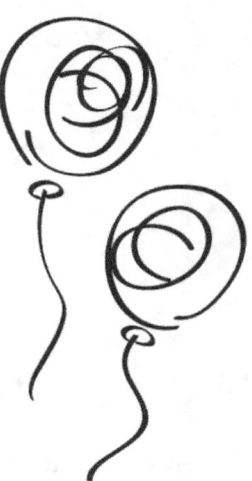

What is success in Canada for you?
Do you want to find a good job?
Do you want to speak English or French (or both) fluently?
Do you want a big house, a good car, or a million dollars in the bank?
Do you want to be happy?

Define WHAT you want. Picture what it looks and feels like.

If you want a good job, clarify what "good" means to you.
Picture where you work, what you do, the people you work with, how much money you make, what you wear to work, where you go for vacation and so on.

To reach a goal, you need to imagine that goal in detail. Visualize it. It could be in the form of an orderly list you can check off as completed. It could be a sentence you post on the wall of your bedroom. It could be a board filled with pictures that reflect your dream.

What your success looks and feels like?

-
-
-

Make it visual, and place it somewhere where you will see it often.

I remember a day when I went to a free workshop held by Toronto Public Health. It was a warm and sunny spring day. The event was set in one of the towers in the heart of downtown Toronto. During lunch time, I went outside and saw beautiful people in beautiful clothes eating their lunches. Their faces were touched tenderly by the sun; they were enjoying the spring warmth, laughing at each other's jokes, and they looked very happy.

I sat near them, enjoying the spring day and the opportunity to vicariously join their ritual of pleasure as I nibbled on an apple I had brought from home. Unlike them, I didn't have any work to go back to after lunch, but I enjoyed the break in that inner courtyard between skyscrapers. They never knew how much I enjoyed that moment of belonging.

And guess what? On every sunny day after that, I closed my eyes and let the sun to touch my face. I smiled and pictured myself back in that courtyard...

And now, I do work in downtown Toronto!

The Sky is no Longer the Limit

It takes a lot of determination, enthusiasm, self-discipline and effort to make your dreams come true.

But FIRST - you have to have a dream!

Chapter 4

CLAIM YOUR RIGHT TO BE HAPPY

We were born to be happy.

Do you feel happy now? Why? Why not?

-
-

What do you need to be happy right at this moment?

-
-
-

Let me tell you a story about one girl…

There was a little girl. She was sitting in her bedroom dreaming. She was dreaming about the time when her mom was alive and they were a big happy family.

That time had passed, but she still loved coming back to those memories. Those memories gave her a warm feeling of belonging, felling needed and being loved.

A couple of years later, memories of day trips, family gatherings, baking and singing together faded away, and it became more and more difficult to find happiness in the past.

But she wanted to be happy…

So - she started living in the future. She pictured things and events that could make her happy: going to summer camp, wearing a beautiful dress, eating chocolate and oranges at winter celebrations and going to a musical.

Soon enough she realized that getting things she was dreaming about didn't make her happy.

She kept dreaming and creating her desired reality, but she also started looking around to see how other people defined happiness.

She read a lot of books and took notes. She found out what others thought about happiness, but she could not relate to any of them. She read definitions over and over until she forgot the most important thing - that she was born to be happy.

She was twelve when her dad remarried and her life became a fairytale. The Cinderella one...

Many years have passed since that time, and now that little girl knows what true happiness means. She has her own definition of happiness.

She still likes to visit her past. She remembers again and again the events and places she went, the people she met, the food she ate and the thoughts and feelings she had.

She still enjoys thinking about her future and picturing the life she will have in five, ten, even fifty years from now.

But most of the time she spends in the present. She lives every minute of her life to the fullest. She doesn't spend every day as if it was her last - she still goes to work, cleans her house and goes to the dentist - but she truly feels every minute of her life.

She has experienced a wild range of feelings: from hate to love, from fear to courage, from tension to serenity. She has many roles in her life, like we all do. She is a child, a parent, a spouse, a friend and an employee. But no matter what role she plays, she never forgets to be happy.

We were born to be happy. Happiness is our birthright. Never let anyone, including yourself, take that away.

You don't need much to be happy if you invite happiness into your life.

Bill Keane said: "Yesterday's the past, tomorrow's the future, but today is a gift. That's why it's called the present."

Listen to yourself. What do you feel now? If you sense nothing, allow yourself to feel.

Denial of pain, sadness, grief, and unhappiness will not make these go away. You need to experience them fully before they can diminish and eventually leave.

Free yourself to experience happiness.

Think about what you do when you are happy: do you smile, sing a song, dance, smell flowers or jump? Do things that make you happy first, and then happiness will come knocking at your door.

Spread happiness all around you. Give away smiles, compliments and positive energy. These will come back to you enhanced. Tell your loved ones: "I love you", write a personal note, bring flowers or make a special meal. Do something you enjoy and invite people to join your festivity!

And you know what? Nobody cares if you can't dance well. Just get up and dance!

Chapter 5

TAKE CARE

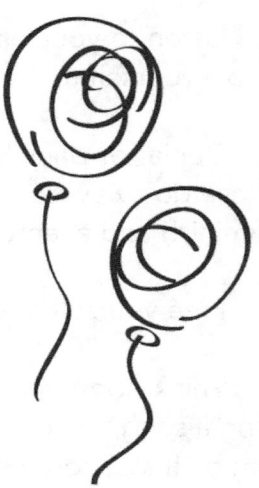

M illions of people live on this planet.

Some days you can feel insignificant and lost in the crowd.

But remember that you could be the world to one.

Please take a minute and think about five important people/ things in your life that you need to take care of.

- ︶
- ︶
- ︶
- ︶
- ︶

Now, look at your work and give yourself a hug if you put yourself in the first place.

Don't be discouraged – almost nobody puts themselves there. You are not alone.

I remember times when taking a long shower and having a hot cup of tea were a luxury I would not allow myself.

Take a look and see if you put yourself on the list at all. You didn't? That's OK too. You are not alone here either.

It's common for humans to take care of others. First we take care of important people and matters; then we take care of secondary people and matters; and finally we think about taking care of ourselves.

It's a common habit, but not a good one. In order to take care of the people on your list, you need to take care of yourself first. It's not selfish!

Taking care of ourselves takes courage, commitment and willingness. Our lives are busy and it's not so easy to keep a commitment to self-care.

Remember - we deserve to take care of ourselves. It not only nourishes us, but also allows us to be available for important matters and people in our lives.

I am not asking you to do a lot. Maybe just spend a few minutes a day.

Stop running, and listen to your heart.

Find a spot where you can be alone. Make yourself comfortable. Slow down and ask: "How am I feeling? How am I really feeling? What makes me feel that way? What makes me happy?"

Take a few minutes every day to do something that makes you and your body happy.

No one else knows you better than you. And if you don't take care of yourself, nobody else will.

Remember, in order to care for someone else, you need to care about yourself first.

Now, please take a minute to list (once again) the important people/things in your life you need to take care of.

-
-
-
-
-

Chapter 6

BE REGRET FREE

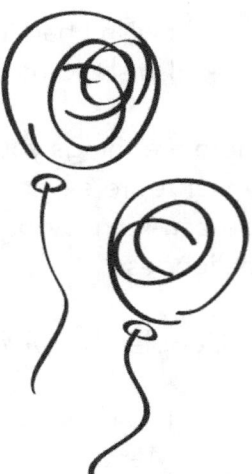

If you had an opportunity to talk to your ten-year-old self, what advice would you give?

I would tell myself to play more; to stop and enjoy the moment I was in; and to stop wishing to be old enough to do more sophisticated things.

Some friends I asked shared that they wished they had taken vocal lessons or attended music classes. They wished they had pursued what they loved the most, such as dancing. They wished they had spent more time with friends. And some wished they had allowed themselves to be natural and stop pretending to be something they were not.

We have so many regrets.

Some time ago, I came across a study which was about the regrets of people who were dying. Here is what they said:

- I wish I had not work so hard
- I wish I had stayed in touch with friends

- I wish I had let myself be happier
- I wish I'd had the courage to express my true self

There are things you can do every day to make sure you don't have similar regrets when the time comes to look back on your life. And you can start by building the resiliency you need to manage life's challenges.

People who live full and happy lives have four types of resiliencies:

- Physical
- Mental
- Emotional
- Social

Everyday do something in each of these categories in order to live longer and have no regrets at the end of your life.

Physical – don't sit still – move around.

At work, I spend a lot of time sitting at my desk. Instead of having a big bottle of water, I switched it to a glass of water and promised myself to get up and refill it every time it was empty. This small adjustment in my everyday routine made a big difference in my physical state. I got more fit – and that feels good!

For your healthy **Mental** state you need to accomplish something every day. It could be something big like getting a new job or taking an exam, or something small like watering a plant.

Every morning I do 15 minutes of exercise. It feels so great when the day has not even started yet and I have already accomplished something.

For the **Emotional** state - do something every day that gives you a good feeling: playing with the kids, walking your dog, listening to music, reading a book, etc.

Social – some days you don't want to talk to or see anyone. Even so, try to say "Thank you" every day to someone you know, or to a stranger. When you make someone's day, your days will get better too.

Most of the time, we regret the things we didn't do even more than the things we did.

I did not tell that person how sorry I am.
I did not try my best in a school competition.
I did not apply for that job.

When that happens, we are filled with regret. But it doesn't have to be like that.

Now I understand this and make different choices. I make the choice to DO rather than NOT DO.

I prefer to live a life of "Oh Wells" instead of "What ifs".

What about you?

List the things you regret about your life:

✓

✓

✓

What would you like to start doing differently now?

⌣

⌣

⌣

Why?

⌣

⌣

⌣

How?

⌣

⌣

⌣

Chapter 7

FIND YOURSELF

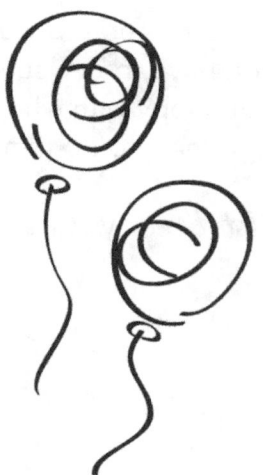

You have all the reasons in the world to feel lost.
You have changed countries; you moved to another continent; you are in a new language environment; the weather, people and culture areall different.

You may feel lost, but now you have a chance to find yourself: the real You. There are few people with expectations of you. You can be whoever you want. You can do whatever you choose. You can have everything you want. You deserve it.

This is a great time to start fresh and find yourself.

We are born with a purpose. When you were a kid, you knew exactly what you wanted to be and to do. Probably you still remember what you dreamed of. However your parents' expectations, social responsibility, fear of disapproval and the desire to be "normal", all made you into someone else.

It is safer to be just like everybody else. In order to be successful you have to get out of your comfort zone and take risks. If you are not happy with who you are, what you do or who you are with, start right now to do things differently.

List things you enjoy doing:

-
-
-

Look at the list and think about how often you do these things.

List things you do not enjoy doing.

-
-
-

Take a look at them too and consider how often you do them.

Pause for a minute and ask yourself why you spend most of your life doing things you do not like? Why do you put on hold all the things you enjoy and keep saying that one day you will do them? How long are you planning to wait? When you win a lottery? When you retire? When your kids grow older?

How about now?

Jim Rohn said: "If you don't design your own life plan, chances are you'll fall into someone else's plan. And guess what they have planned for you? Not much."

Plan your life. Find what you want and where you are going. Love what you do and believe in yourself!

Now is a first day of the rest of your life!

No other person knows you better. Get your creative thinking going. Ask yourself: "What is good in my life? What else could be done?"

Be honest with yourself. Honesty is beautiful. Truth leads you to clarity and self-motivation.

I love my work. It incorporates many things I enjoy doing: empowering people through education, developing learning events, meeting new people and travelling. But, I also enjoy being at home with my kids, I like long walks in early mornings, I like reading while swinging in a hammock in shade of a big tree, I enjoy gardening and doing yoga…

For a long time I thought I could not change anything. Moreover, I did not feel that I needed to change anything. I would go to work every workday. I would come home and have an hour or two with the kids before they fell asleep. I would read in the train. I would try to fit in what I enjoy between shopping, cleaning and cooking. I squeezed everything in like this because I was planning for early retirement.

Do I need to wait another twenty years? Why not fit everything I love doing into my everyday life?

Now I have a plan.

How about you?

Chapter 8

WHO MAKES YOUR CHOICES?

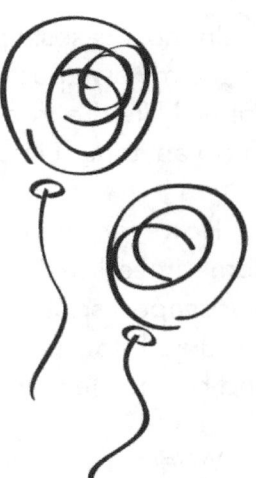

I used to think that I would never drive a car. Partially because back home a car was not thought of as a means of transportation but as a luxury; partially because of the aggressive driving I witnessed on the roads; and lastly, because I was afraid to sit behind the wheel of a car and drive faster than I can run.

Now, driving is an essential part of my everyday life, and I'm glad I decided to take that risk and face my fear.

Since I have been driving for many hours every week, I have experienced many types of roads. I classify them into three categories:

City roads – these roads have a fair surface, clear lines, and many stop signs, traffic lights, pedestrians and cyclists.

Highways – these roads have a good surface, clear lines, no stop signs, no traffic lights, no pedestrians, no cyclists and no distractions.

Country roads - have poor pavement, limited lane separation, few stop signs, rare traffic lights and few pedestrians.

In most cases, I prefer to take the highways in my life. I prefer to create my own path and not be restricted by speed limits and traffic lights. I like the freedom my imagination can offer and the freedom to do anything I imagine.

However, there are times when I choose to take other roads. Sometimes I like to take country roads and experience beautiful landscapes, spot wild animals, meet strangers and find myself in the middle of nowhere. This opens up new horizons, new perspectives and brings me new stories and experiences.

When I feel emotionally exhausted, I avoid the highway. I take time to recover and rest on a country road. This gives me time to think, without the pressure of speed. Taking it slow when I need to helps me go as far as I want and as high as I envision.

As for the city roads, these I take when I want company and lots of stimulation (and I have no need for convenient parking!)

Whatever you may have been taught about which road is better, smoother, safer or faster; you need to choose your own way. Your life, your choice, your road!

Chapter 9

MAKE YOUR OWN NEWS

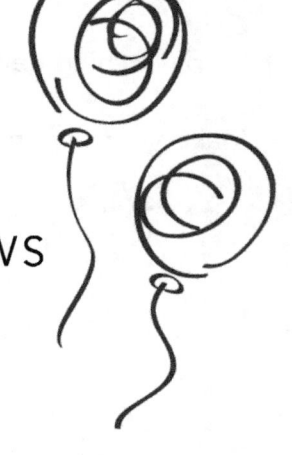

I do not watch TV.

When I tell people this, most of the time they look puzzled, feel sorry for me and ask if it is by choice.

Yes, - this is a conscious decision. We choose not to have TV at home.

Some time ago I realized that watching the news did not make me happy: advertisements affected my mind and made me hungry for junk food; and the unreal lives life of soap opera characters took over MY life. They had fun and I was watching. They fell in love and I was watching. They achieved something and I was (again), watching. My life was on hold because I was too busy following theirs.

I deprogrammed myself and chose to live life on my side of the screen. I started looking into my life, watching what happened to me every day. I filled up my life with my own news. I finally woke up and started living my OWN life!

Do you want to sleep better, eat better, live better?

Stop watching news!

Make your own news and choose on which side of the screen you want to live!

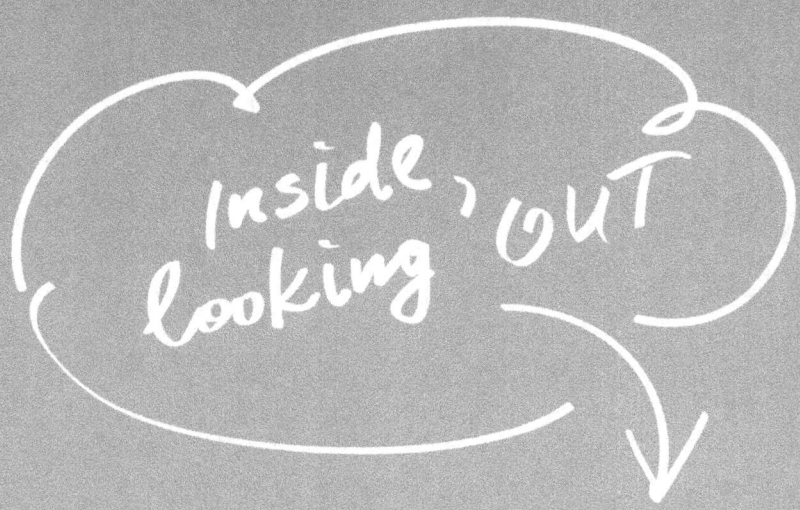

Who you are inside is not the whole equation.
The way you share yourself with the world
and how you connect with the world
also matters. To succeed you must know yourself
and, more importantly, be yourself, no matter
what the rest of the world thinks.

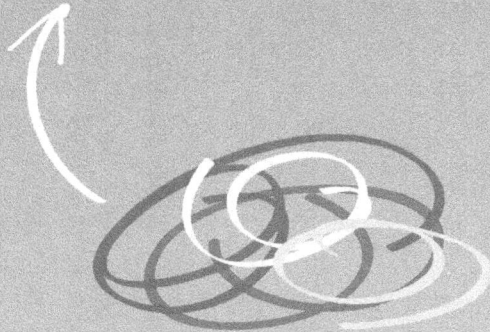

"Be yourself. The world worships the original".
Ingrid Bergman

Chapter 10

WHAT DO YOU THINK OF ME?

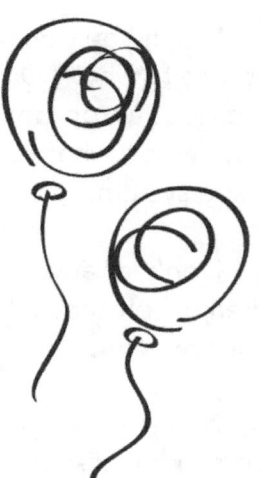

When I was younger, I constantly worried about what others thought of me. I worried about how I looked and what I said or didn't say. Because of this, I had a difficult time saying "No".

Part of this tendency was cultural; the other part was a natural desire to be loved by everyone.

I did everything to please the people around me, without paying attention to whether it was actually good or convenient for me. People took advantage of my kindness and often took me for granted.

No matter how hard I tried, I still found that not everybody liked me, which stressed me out. Sometime later I heard the expression - "I am not a $100 bill that everyone automatically likes!" I stopped and reflected on the hidden message and finally gave myself permission to put myself and my own welfare first.

It takes time and effort to discover and trust your internal guidance system.

When you decide to do something or not to do something, ask yourself "why"? Does it come from fear of what others will think? If it does - stop doing (or not doing) it immediately! Listen to your gut and do what you feel needs to be done, according to your own value system.

Don't let anyone tell that you can't do something - if you have a dream – protect it. Don't let anyone stand in the way of you fulfilling your passion.

Never lower your standards or expectations just because one person has disappointed you. The decision about who you want to share your journey with is yours alone.

Whatever you are feeling at any given moment is a perfect reflection of where you are in the process of becoming who you are.

Not believing in your own abilities is one of the most harmful things that you can do to yourself. There are always things we know and things we don't know. Once you believe that you can learn the things you don't know, you will succeed. People will trust you if you trust yourself. When you don't trust yourself, your life becomes an endless waiting game for someone to change the things that are actually yours to fix.

Have high hopes and act upon them.
Be open to everything and attached to nothing!

Don't waste your energy trying to change how others see you.

What do you think of ME?
You know what? That is none of my business.

Chapter 11

BE OPEN TO OPPORTUNITIES

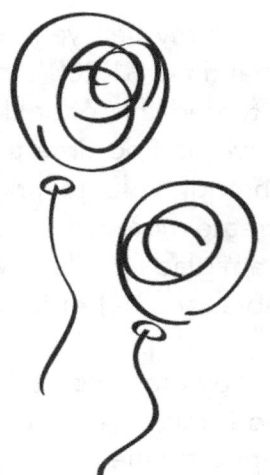

Opportunities come and go. Some you notice, some you don't. Some you take advantage of and some you don't.

Be available mentally and physically for opportunities. Keep your mind open to them. Two people dealing with the same situation may have different outcomes. One could be complaining of inconvenience, the other might contemplate how to change things for the better. That is how many inventions were created.

Sleep is very important. Make sure you get enough sleep. When you are awake, be alert every minute of your life. Be in the moment, ask questions and discover answers.

Remember - in order to find an answer, you need to first form a question.
Be alert and curious.

When an opportunity shows itself, look at it from different angles. Money is only one thing to consider.

In my first year in Canada, I was offered a babysitting job. At that time, $1,200 a month looked like a pretty good deal. However, I turned this offer down as it would take up all my time. I would have had no time to work on my English, explore the community through volunteering or to attend courses, which could ultimately create more options. It was not an easy decision to make, but now I am glad I made it. We had to keep our life very simple to be available for a better future.

By grasping at the first opportunity without thinking it through, you might end up rejecting or leaving no space for future opportunities.

For example, looking for a job is a full-time job in itself. You need time to commit to the following time consuming tasks:

- ✓ Daily searching for job postings.
- ✓ Adapting your resume and cover letter to each position.
- ✓ Working on your skills to be more employable.
- ✓ Attending events in your professional area.
- ✓ Meeting people and building your network.

I recognize that you may face a situation where you have to work at any job, as long as it brings in some money. However, in the back of your mind, you always need a plan for how to find a better one.

Ask yourself: do I really need a survival job? Do I have enough money to live on?

If you know you can hold out for a better opportunity, or even if you have to take that survival job today, make a list of what you need to do to find a better job.

When creating your list, consider the following:

- What are my gaps in knowledge, experience, and skills?
- How can I improve them?
- What professional courses can I take?
- How can I meet people in my profession?
- When and how will I look for job postings?
- What employment courses are available?
- Do I need help to create a resume?

Make a list of what you need to do to find a good job:

✓

✓

✓

Then think about how you will act on it.

Do not put it on hold or say that "someday I will do it". Do something from your list every day. Ask your family or friends to help.

My husband found a job in his profession. It had very low pay and was located far away from home. But this job provided invaluable job experience — CANADIAN job experience. The downside was that it left no time in the day to look for other work.

I offered my help, and spent a few hours a day looking for job postings on job search websites. I had no specific knowledge of the job requirements of his profession; however, I was able to match the skills my husband has with the skills employers were looking for.

By the time he arrived home each day, I had 30-40 postings selected. He looked them over, found three to five good matches, altered his resume and sent it out.

Look for help from your relatives, friends, and even your children. You never know what they might come up with!

My husband also benefitted from the knowledge, skills and resources I acquired while attending employment courses. I helped him prepare for his interviews by learning about each prospective employer, reviewing possible questions, designing the best answers and then practicing with him. We built on each other. Without each other the journey would not have been so fulfilling and successful!

You too are not alone.

Chapter 12

THE POWER OF NO

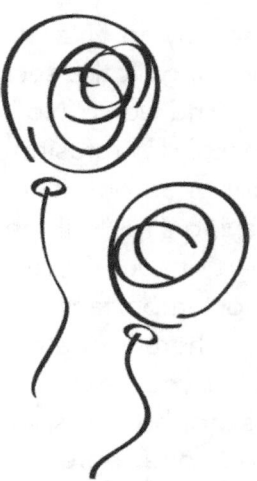

Knowing how to say "No" is vital to your success. You needed to learn to say "No".

Sometimes it's tough to determine which activities deserve your time and attention. Say "Yes" to activities that support your focus and say "No" to things which are not associated with it. Ask yourself if the new commitment is important to you. If it's something you feel strongly about, by all means do it. If not, take a pass. There are some things you can never get back: your time, your health, and your life. Be wise when saying "Yes" and adding extra stress to your life.

Also, it is better to say "No", than to say "Yes" and not follow through. Do you want to be one of those people who say "Yes" to everything and in the end do almost nothing?

If you have to say "No", just say "No".
Be mindful of persuasion techniques that people often use when asking. And don't let them game you. You may need to refuse a request several times before the other person accepts your response. When that happens, just hit the replay button. Be mindful

that saying "No" the first time makes you more likely to say "Yes" out of guilt the second time.

The word "No" has power. Don't be afraid to use it. State your reason for refusing the request, but don't fabricate reasons to get out of an obligation. Saying "No" won't be easy if you're used to saying "Yes" all the time. But learning to say "No" is an important part of your success since you get more time for the things that are most important to you.

There is one more thing I would like to say about "No".

If you hear a sincere, personal "No" from someone when you ask for help; respect it. But, if that "No" comes from the system or someone representing the system, it is just a bureaucratic "No". In Canada, you have the right to challenge the system if it doesn't work for you.

So, when you are trying to open the door to new opportunities, tasting the possibilities or simply learning about things – do not take this "No" for an answer. If you hear "No" – keep asking. Ask the same question more than once at different times and in different situations.

When I was considering becoming a Public Health Nurse – a Nurse who works with community to promote the health and prevent illnesses - people often told me that I would never get it. They said it is very difficult to get in, especially for someone educated internationally.

I took "No" as a challenge. You are saying that I won't become who I want to be because someone considers it VERY DIFFICULT? Can't you be more creative than that?

I challenged the system, I applied, I went through an interview and I won. I become a Public Health Nurse!

Do what you feel is right for you and don't let any "No" stop you.

The Sky is no Longer the Limit

Initiative is one of the most powerful skills you can have. Do not be afraid to think differently or start project of your own. Do not be afraid to push against the system if it doesn't make sense to you. And once you start, keep going. Always strive to do your best.

Chapter 13

BE OPTIMISTIC

I am an optimist. I believe that I can do anything if I put my mind to it and pursue it. I believe I can shape my own future.

Do you feel the same way? Why? Why not?

-
-
-

When you wake up every day you have two choices - you can face the world positively or negatively - it's all a matter of perspective. I choose to be an optimist. I think creatively and take action. I challenge any problem I face, and I believe that every difficulty has a great gift hidden inside it.

When I decided to get my license as a Registered Nurse in Ontario, I learned that the regulatory body did not recognize my nursing education and suggested that I go back to school. I love studying but the thought of studying the same subjects all over again, was daunting.

I stood up for myself and told them that that I thought my education and experience should be recognized. That's when I learned that there is a process to follow to have my credentials approved. I followed the process, and in the end, my education and experience were recognized by the governing body. I was granted permission to take the nursing exam without additional education.

Do your research. Ask questions. Find answers. Fulfill your dreams.

Finding the bright side of a tough situation motivated me to take a risk. As a result I now have my RN credentials in Canada. As well, this challenging experience with the regulatory body served me well in obtaining a job at York University - first helping Internationally Educated Nurses, and later managing the project.

Optimism can be acquired at any age. Understand that it may not be your fault if you are knocked down, but it is certainly your fault if you don't get up.

The way you react to reality is who you become. Your mental attitude defines your success. It is never too late to start working on your attitude.

Try these strategies for successful optimism:

- ✓ Surround yourself with positive and successful people.
- ✓ Observe and remember what they do and how they do it.
- ✓ Don't be jealous of others' success – instead, visualize your own success.

- Avoid negativity and people who lower your self-esteem.
- Don't blame others for your failures and don't take your failures personally.
- Face fears and deal with them.
- Start slowly - change one thought at a time.
- Get out of your comfort zone and try things you are afraid of.
- Take responsibility for your own life – the only person responsible for your life is YOU.
- Accept yourself as you are. You are enough to generate your own happiness.

The happiest people in the world are those who are responsible for their own happiness. Take it easy. Do not expect others to be perfect and allow yourself to make mistakes too. There's not just one way to do things right.

Chapter 14

SERVE AND GET FULFILLED

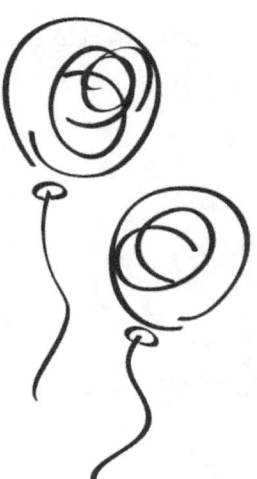

Do things for others. Create success in your life by offering something of value for free.

When you offer something without really expecting anything in return, people have a special gratitude for you. And that gratitude is transformed into truthful promotion of your work.

Passion is Energy! Having passion for everything I do has made the difference in my life. The more passionate you are about yourself, your work, your life or whatever it is you are doing…the more positive energy you give away. And as you know - the more you give, the more you receive!

Passion is something you feel deep in your heart. Passion is an intense emotion that gives you energy to work or play, day or night.

List things that you enjoy doing:

-
-
-

How can what you enjoy serve others?

-
-
-

Be honest with yourself. Be open to new experiences as they can enlighten and improve you.

Find a volunteer placement that you can fulfill with your passion.

I have a friend who is passionate about helping people to get better. She is a nurse and, while she was waiting for her nursing license, she found a placement at the Hospital in a program helping patients to recover through communication with animals.

I have another friend who wanted to find a volunteer position to improve his language skills without him offering match in return. He never got one.

Be passionate about what you do. Believe in yourself and in your service or product. Find a way for your passion to help others. Share your knowledge. Offer encouragement. Become a mentor…

Serve – be fulfilled – and become successful!

Chapter 15

BITE OFF AS MUCH AS YOU CAN CHEW

Coming to Canada, we faced many challenges. One of them is a very different lifestyle.

I remember being surprised by seeing two or three cars in the driveway of a small house. I was astonished by coffee shops and eateries that were busy in the middle of a weekday.

I was amazed at how Canadians spend money.

These temptations are very contagious. They grab you and carry you away in a merry dance. But after a while, you find yourself with accumulated debts, having to work long hours just to pay bills.

You may not be able to afford a nice trip on the water, because you are too busy paddling against the current. Paddle, paddle, paddle…8 to 12 hours a day, every day, no vacations, no holidays, no sick days…a mortgage, car loan, insurance, property taxes, utility bills, restaurants, clothing, iPad, iPod, iPhone…paddle, paddle,

paddle...look straight, concentrate, a short break and again...paddle, paddle, paddle...

Do you want to be on that boat?

Are you already there?

It is difficult to get off that boat, but you always have a choice. If you could choose to jump into spending mode, you can also choose to go back to a simpler life.

Don't look for excuses, like saying that your kids need this and that. Many of us grew up living in small apartments, with few toys and limited food choices.

You may think that kids need many things, but what is needed most is quality time spent together with family. By working on survival jobs, you are losing out on both your career and your family life. You make a little money to make ends meet. But you are tired, unsatisfied and unfulfilled, and that brings unhappiness into your family relationships.

Don't try to keep up with the rest of the world. You still will not have everything you want. Be patient. Do what is right for you now.

You need a place to live. You need to eat, dress, commute and stay connected.

Rent a place to live until you are certain that you can afford to buy one. Use public transportation instead of owning a car. Limit eating out and make your own food. Be strong and do not take on more than you can manage. Do not try to fit into anybody else's picture of happiness.

Instead of buying stuff, buy time off for yourself. In order to be successful, you need time. You need time to look around and adjust, to find what you want to do, to identify your weaknesses and work on them. You need time to invest in yourself; to work on your professional and personal development; and to sharpen your ability to communicate and navigate through the system.

Keep your luggage light and have minimum financial responsibilities.
Be modest and spend wisely.

Go out, meet people, and experience Canada and its culture.

Canada offers hundreds of free events: festivals, parades, museum visits, classes for adults and kids, open door events, music in the park, movies under the stars, and much more. You do not need to spend a penny to have fun. You just need to have love in your heart, some food and a bottle of water in your backpack.

What do your expenses look like now?

-
-
-

What percentage of your income goes to cover your monthly expenses?

⌣

How can you modify your expenses to have more flexibility with your money?

⌣

⌣

⌣

Do you think money is the way to happiness, or the cause of all problems?
    Do you believe that money is your birthright, or do you feel that you do not deserve it?
    Do you like to think about money, or does it make you nervous?

    Your money beliefs are developed in your childhood.

What is your earliest money experience?

⌣

⌣

⌣

What your parents favorite saying about money:

- ✓
- ✓
- ✓

You may not consciously agree with the money beliefs of your family; however, they are still the beliefs that pop into your mind first. For example:

- ✓ Money often costs too much.
- ✓ Money is the root of all evil.
- ✓ Those who have the gold make the rules.
- ✓ A penny saved is a penny earned.
- ✓ A good reputation is more valuable than money.
- ✓ The rich get richer, and the rest of us feel lucky to find a quarter on the sidewalk.

Your beliefs and attitudes are shaped by these childhood messages.

My family's favorite saying was:
"Money attracts money and we don't have any."

So we never had enough to have a comfortable life. When I left my family home and started living on my own, I never had enough money either, no matter how hard I worked.

We had a very simple lifestyle and I was taught to live within my means. I rarely borrowed money and if I did, I paid it back from my next pay cheque.

When we came to Canada, we had a plan to keep it simple and not get into debt. We managed it well in our first year, but then we had a life lesson which changed our financial viewpoint.

My husband and I decided to rent a car to travel outside of Toronto for a day trip. As it turned out, we couldn't rent a car because we didn't have a credit card. That was a turning point for me: I had to start educating myself about personal finances.

I quickly learned that in order to borrow something (a car, money to buy a house, "buy now pay later" plans for furniture, etc.), you must have a good credit score.

A credit score is a numerical expression created to evaluate the potential risk of lending you money. It can range from 300-900; where 560-659 is fair; 660-724 is good; and 725-759 is very good.

You can request a free copy of your credit file or purchase your credit score report from Equifax.

What goes into credit score numbers?

35% of your credit score is based on your payment history – missing payments hurts your score more than anything else.

30% is based on credit utilization – what percentage of your available credit you are using. It is best to be using less than 30% because it shows that you know how to use credit wisely.

15% of the score is based on the length of your credit history – how long ago you opened the credit accounts and how active they are. They are looking for evidence of regular and responsible use of credit.

10% of your credit rating comes from the amount of new credit you have – what accounts were opened recently and how many recent inquiries were made on your account. Too many inquiries can lower this score.

10% of your score is based on how many different types of credit you have. It is better to have various types of credit.

Some things to remember:

- ✓ Pay all your bills on time. One late payment can drop your score more than twenty points!

- ✓ Monitor your credit report every year. If you notice activities that do not belong to you, contact the credit bureau and have them check it out.

- ✓ Never close your oldest account and do not cancel your oldest credit card.

I was scared to borrow money, but I learned that I would have to borrow in order to fully participate in Canadian society.

Do you know that not all debt is bad? Good debt, such as a mortgage or a student loan, is an investment in your future. Bad debt, such as credit-card debt or a car loan, does not help you make money later and will put you further in the hole.

"A bank is a place that will lend you money if you can prove that you don't need it." – Bob Hope

So…in order to borrow money, you have to show that you know how to handle money, and that you always pay it back.

Write down all your debts (line of credit accounts, credit cards, car loans, etc.), and the amounts you owe on each of them:

-
-
-
-
-

Chapter 16

WHAT IS YOUR MONEY PSYCHOLOGY?

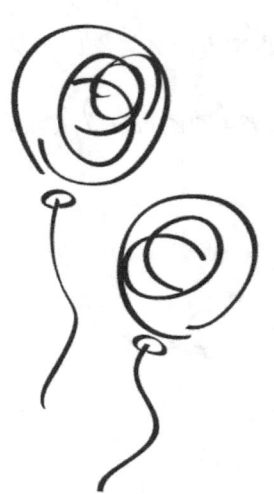

Do you believe that money is a source of happiness?

Do you feel that money makes life easier?
Do you see money as a positive reward for your hard work?

You may find yourself being obsessed about money. You may look at every decision through a money filter. For example when you have two job offers, you may automatically choose the one that pays more without looking at the opportunities the other job could offer. An obsession with money can also make you cheap.

Do you believe that money is a source of stress?

You may feel that you will never have enough, so why even try?

Or, you may think that having a lot of money is a problem in itself.

You may feel that money is not important, so you don't respect it.

You may avoid financial risk, or increase it by missing payments or refusing to deal with money problems.

You may be too cheap or overly private about your finances.

No matter what your personal money psychology, and no matter what money beliefs you bring from your past, you likely give money a lot of emotional value and power. Most people do.

You need balance in your financial life. To get it, you may have to reconsider what you think and feel about money.

Money is a tool. You can manage it well or poorly.

Do you find yourself in the dark about your financial future?
Are you ignoring how you will pay for your children's education?
Are you saving money for retirement?
Do you rush into financial decisions?
Are you using tomorrow's money to pay for today?
Are you always comparing yourself to others who have more?

If you answered "Yes" to at least one of these questions, you should consider the following:

Today, you can wake up and start taking control of your finances. It's never too late to start planning for your future.

Common bad money habits:

- Borrowing money from friends and family
- Impulse shopping
- Keeping all your money in a checking account

- Carrying a credit card balance
- Making late payments
- Avoiding writing a will
- Not budgeting
- Procrastinating about investing in your future
- Ignoring your debts
- Not knowing your credit score
- Not having the right insurance
- Trying to maintain a lifestyle you cannot afford.

Write down your bad money habits below:

-
-
-

Good money habits:

- Knowing the balance in your accounts
- Knowing your credit score
- Keeping to a budget
- Having all the insurance you and your dependents need
- Shopping with a list
- Saving money for retirement
- Taking at least 24 hours to think through any significant purchase
- Having and following a financial plan
- Knowing your savings goals
- Always reading the fine print

- ✓ Researching and consulting with objective experts when making significant decisions
- ✓ Not doing something just because everyone else does it
- ✓ Setting goals based on your current situation

Remember that personal finance is not a competitive sport. Everyone's personal finances are unique.

Budgeting

Some people enjoy creating a detailed budget and sticking to it. They track everyday spending and enter it in some kind of summary document. They watch closely what they spend money on and make sure that no dollar is spent on something that was not planned.

Then, there is the rest of the world: the majority of people who don't have a budget. They spend money without planning or tracking and usually buy what they want, when they want it. They may try to live within their means, but rarely know where their money goes.

No matter which group you belong to, you will benefit from the following **magical budgeting formula: 50/20/30**

50% - Essentials – housing/transportation/groceries/utilities

20% - Future – savings for education/emergency/retirement/debt payment

30% - Lifestyle – shopping/restaurants/entertainment/personal care

Using this formula will simplify your detailed entries and help you organize your spending by focusing on these three main categories of spending. If you want to know more, the book, Financially Fearless, by Alexa Von Tobel provides a detailed explanation of this budgeting approach, including many examples and useful tools.

When budgeting, think about the big picture. What do you want to accomplish?

Input your actual numbers then decide how you need to adjust your expenses.

Reflect on the process every three months and make changes as needed.

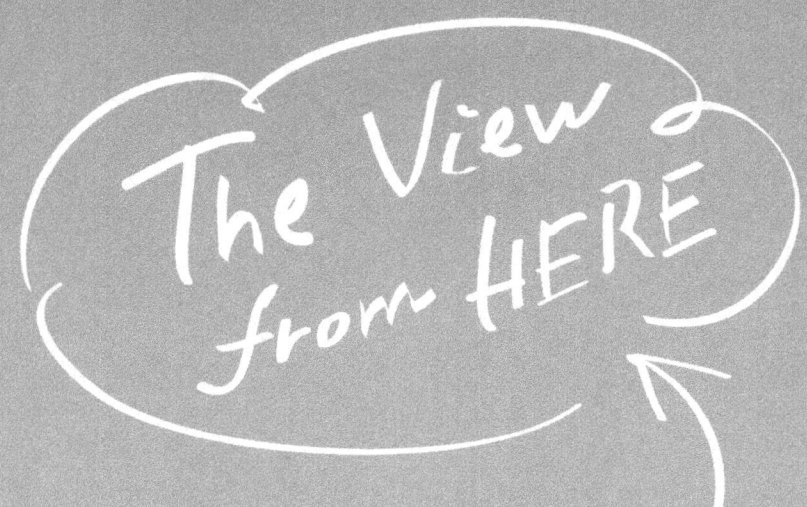

The View from HERE

Right here, right now is your only reality.
Your success depends on who you are, inside and out. But it also depends on how well you embrace the place and the people around you.
Nothing happens in a vacuum.
Become an expert at using all the tools and resources Canada and your community can offer you.
Become an expert at valuing the people you love and rely on every day.

"Wherever you are - be all there".
Jim Elliot

Chapter 17

RESP, RRSP AND MORE

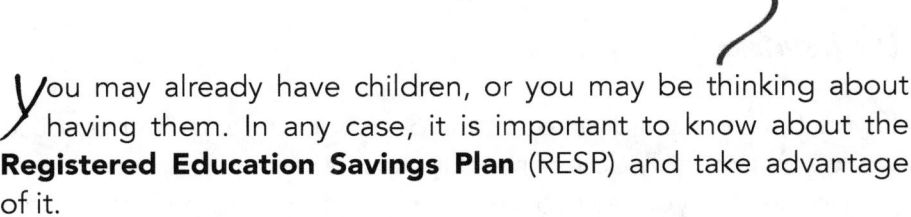

You may already have children, or you may be thinking about having them. In any case, it is important to know about the **Registered Education Savings Plan** (RESP) and take advantage of it.

There are many reasons why an RESP is important, including free money! Here is how it works:

First - you start saving for the education of your children. The earlier you start, the more you save.

Second – each year, the government gives you a grant equal to 20 percent of the amount you saved that year. This is the basic Canada Education Savings Grant (CESG).

Third – you may get even more free money from the government if you are eligible for the supplemental CESG for lower income families. Sometimes, there is even a little more free money available in the form of a Canada Learning Bond (CLB).

In any case, all children up to age 17 are eligible for the Education Grant, as long as they are Canadian residents and an RESP has been opened for them.

While it's in the RESP, the money you invest and the free government contributions grow tax free. Later, your child can use the money for full-time or part-time studies in an apprenticeship program, trade school, college or university.

There are limits to the Education Grant you can receive. For example, this year $500 is the limit for Basic CESG. I contribute $208 per child to take advantage of the full 20 percent available from the government. You can also save more, but additional amounts will not receive the 20 percent government contribution.

You need to consider not only maxing out free money, but also your ability to make the same amount in monthly contributions for many years.

If you feel that $200 a month is not manageable now, or could be challenging in the future, save less. You will still get the 20 percent free money from the government on the amount you do save.

Life insurance

If you have no children or other dependents, and both spouses work, you probably do not need life insurance.

However, if you find yourself in situation where people depend on you financially, you need to make sure you have sufficient life insurance.

The purpose of life insurance is to protect your financial dependents in the event of your death.

There are a number of options for life insurance. For my family, low-cost Term Insurance (temporary insurance that provides higher coverage when you need it most), was the best solution.

But every family and every situation is different, so work with a reputable insurance broker to determine the best life insurance solution to fit your needs.

To get an idea of how much life insurance you will need, do some simple calculations:

- ✓ Determine how much family income you need each year to maintain your current lifestyle.
- ✓ Determine how many years your family will need this income.

- ✓ Determine any major one-time costs or purchases that would happen in the event of your death.
- ✓ Add these numbers together for the minimum amount of life insurance you need.

Don't wait too long. The younger and the healthier you are, the better premium you will qualify for.

Plan for retirement

Canada's retirement income system has three levels:

Old Age Security (OAS) provides the first level, or foundation. If you meet certain residence requirements, you will be entitled to a modest monthly pension once you reach the age of 65. This retirement income foundation also includes a Guaranteed Income Supplement (GIS) for those who have no other forms of retirement income.

Note: The age of eligibility for Old Age Security (OAS) pension and the Guaranteed Income Supplement (GIS) will gradually increase from 65 to 67 over six years, starting in April 2023.

The Canada Pension Plan (CPP) is the second level of the system. It provides you with a monthly retirement pension as early as 60, if you have paid into it. The amount of the benefit depends on three factors: how long you have paid into the plan; how much you have paid into the plan; and whether you start receiving your CPP benefit early (before age 65) or late (after age 65). The Canada Pension Plan also offers disability, survivor and death benefits. Quebec has a similar plan, called the Quebec Pension Plan.

The third level of the retirement income system consists of private pensions and personal savings.

The first and second levels of Canada's retirement income system make up Canada's public pension system. Today, these pensions form a significant part of the income of Canada's seniors. But public pensions are not intended to meet all your financial needs in retirement. Rather, they provide a modest base for you to build upon with additional, **private savings**.

You have to get into the right state of mind before you can accumulate wealth. Many people can't decide whether to move forward or backward and, as result, they remain stuck and don't do anything at all.

Some feel that it is too early to start saving for retirement and some conclude that it is too late…neither is true.

There are a few ways to save for your retirement and I encourage you to explore your options.

Take advantage of employer and government programs.

About 40 percent of workers in Canada are covered by an employer pension plan, formally called **Registered Pension Plans (RPPs).**

If you are one of the 40 percent, review your company's pension booklet. It explains the terms of your employer pension plan. Find out what kind of plan you have and ask about the age of normal (and early) retirement.

Take a look at the statement of benefits for your work pension plan. This statement contains information such as your credited years or service, employee and employer contributions during the year, the pension benefit earned during the year and your expected retirement date.

Registered Retirement Savings Plans (RRSPs)

RRSPs are the most effective and popular way to build personal savings for retirement, especially if you don't participate in an employer pension plan.

RRSPs are individual, personally managed savings plans. Like the employer pension, savings in an RRSP receive tax assistance: contributions are tax deductible and investment income is not taxed as it is earned. The tax is paid when funds are withdrawn from these plans.

These following two programs: **The Home Buyers' Plan (HBP)** and **The Lifelong Learning Plan (LLP)** allow you to withdraw money from your RRSP without immediate tax consequences.

The HPB allows withdrawals of up to $25,000 for the down payment on your first home. After taking the money out using either of these two plans, you must return the amount withdrawn in 10 (for LLP) or 15 (for HPB) years.

The following example shows how I saved money for my first house using my RRSP.

In my first job I learned that my Employer was matching employees' contributions towards an RRSP. I started contributing $150 a month and my employer added another $150 each month to my RRSP account.

My next job didn't offer a pension plan, but my salary was higher. I increased my RRSP contribution to $200 a month. When my husband found a better job, and we had more money available, my RRSP contribution gradually reached $1,000 a month. In four years, my RRSP account grew to $30,000

This amount consisted of my investments, my employer's contribution and the interest earned on my account.

Since I didn't pay income tax on my contributions or the interest earned, I also saved about $8,000 over that four year period.

One small first step of putting aside $150 a month allowed me to develop the good habit of saving that built a foundation for the down payment on our family home. I took advantage of the Home Buyers' Plan and withdrew $25,000.

Tax Free Savings Account (TFSA)

A TFSA is one last personal savings program that can help you save for your retirement (or any other financial goal). The government describes a TFSA as a "flexible, registered, general-purpose savings plan that allows Canadians to earn tax-free investment income to more easily meet lifetime savings needs. The TFSA complements existing registered savings plans like the Registered Retirement Savings Plans (RRSP) and the Registered Education Savings Plans (RESP)."

For you, a TFSA is just one more way to make your savings dollars work harder.

One year after coming to Canada, we had only $100. It was difficult to imagine that we would be driving good cars and living in our own house a few years later.

Remember, your dreams have no limit. No matter how much money you have in your pocket - you have unlimited wealth in your mind.

Enjoy what you have, take pleasure in the goals you have accomplished and look forward the bright future that awaits you!

Chapter 18

HAVE PEACE OF MIND

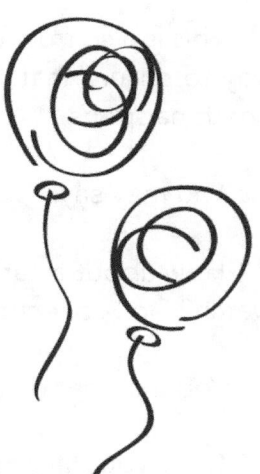

*H*ave you ever felt that you wanted to do something very important, but you had run out of time?

I felt that way not long ago, when I realized that time was short and there were some things I wished I'd done. One of these things was writing a will. I have two kids, and I wanted to make sure that even if I was gone, their lives would continue as I intended. I wrote my husband a letter outlining some things that are important to me, including how to access the life insurance policy provided by my workplace and a reminder to him that we also have a term life insurance policy. I listed the schools I had chosen for the kids, suggested some good extracurricular activities, reminded him to keep investing in RESP's, and to continue some traditions such as visiting a café with milk and shortbread cookies after a doctor's appointment.

I knew that he would take good care of the kids, yet writing a letter sharing these thoughts gave me peace of mind.

If something happens to you, the family you leave behind cannot respect your wishes if they don't know your wishes.

This is also true for your financial wishes. Having a will is the best way to ensure that your plan for distributing your assets after your death happens.

You may say: "I don't own a lot!"

How about a car? What about your books? Paintings? A special watch? Doll collection?

You may be worth more than you think.

Over your lifetime you can build a small fortune. At the end of the day, do you want this to go to your loved ones or the provincial government?

Without a will, the court will designate an executor for you. And the government-appointed executor may or may not be the best person to do the job. A government appointed executor will also charge fees to the estate – leaving less for your family.

A will is a list of the individuals or organizations that will get your assets when you die and how much (or what) will go to each. You may change a will over time as your circumstances change. When you prepare a will, or if you decide to alter your will, you don't have to consult any of the named beneficiaries. However, you should speak to anyone you want to name as an executor or co-executor to make sure they are comfortable with the responsibility. You can name one or more people (over the age of eighteen) as executors. The person you select should be honest and knowledgeable.

If you have children, you can also name a guardian in your will to look after them. When you are deciding on guardians, consider the following:

- ✓ Find a younger couple who will not find it too difficult to take on extra children.

- ✓ Make sure they are willing to bring up your kids if something happens to you and your spouse.
- ✓ Consider their beliefs, parenting style, religion, geographical location etc. and look for someone who will not create too much change in your children's life when they are already coping with loss.

Give yourself peace of mind. If you are 18 years of age or older, make an appointment with a competent lawyer and put your wishes on paper.

One more thing…

As long as you are already consulting a lawyer about a will, be sure to discuss powers of attorney for property and personal care.

A will makes your wishes known if you die. Power of attorney documents provide direction when you are still alive but unable to make decisions for yourself. For example, a power of attorney for property might appoint your spouse or a trusted friend to handle your finances if you were in a car accident that left you in a temporary coma. A power of attorney for personal care would name someone to make decisions about your health and well-being when you can't.

Chapter 19

LIFE IS....

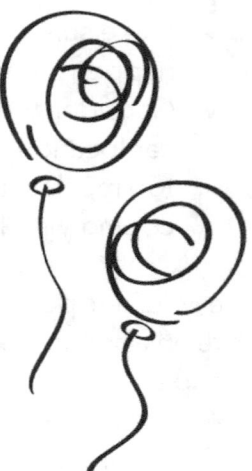

L ife is a journey, a song, a game, a challenge, a dream....
Life is many other things, but life is not a scavenger hunt!

A scavenger hunt is a game in which individuals must find specific items, or perform tasks, as presented on a list.

If life were a scavenger hunt, your life milestones could be listed as follows:

Birth, first breath, first scream, first smile, first tooth, first step, first word. Then kindergarten, grade school, first love, college/university, job, marriage, first house...

Followed by children, grandchildren, great-grandchildren, death....

We all have lists created by society, parents, friends, and even strangers.

One day I was at the museum and saw children running from one room to the other. They were on a mission. They were looking for certain objects in the exhibits. The intent of the creator of this scavenger hunt was to make sure that the children would reach every corner of the museum and experience every collection presented. But instead of seeing what was around them, the children were looking only for the items on the list. As soon as they found one, they ran looking for the next item on the list. In the end, they succeeded with the scavenger hunt activity and had some fun running around, but they did not experience the museum itself.

Does your life feel like a scavenger hunt?

Do you find yourself running from one place to the other?
Do you check one item off the list and run to find the next?

Life is not a scavenger hunt!
Life is an experience - your experience.

Stop and smell the roses!

Stop running and enjoy beauty of life!

Feel the wind on your skin, listen to the birds sing and notice what's going on in front of your eyes.

Life is an adventure…YOUR ADVENTURE.

Get out there and discover it!

Chapter 20

YOU ARE WHAT YOU EAT

Do you want to be healthy?
You are what you eat, think, do and believe.

If you want to be healthy, you need to eat healthy.
You may ask what eating healthy actually means.

For many years I had only one question about food: "how much does it cost?"
The place I am from had very limited food choices and my family could not afford most of them.

When I came to Canada, I was lost in grocery stores. There were so many boxes, cans and bags of food, I could not relate. There were so many fruits and vegetables I was not familiar with; as well as a huge variety of the more recognizable things like apples, potatoes, meat, milk, sour cream, bread and pasta. I was confused - which one to choose?

I learned something new every time I went to the grocery store: new food, new names, new concepts.

"Free run chicken". What does that mean? Were they jailed before, but managed to break free?

"Grass fed beef" What else would they eat?

With such a gigantic variety of food choices, I had difficulty understanding which ones were right for me.

So I went for the low cost items.

It took me a few years to understand what "healthy food" means. I would like to share what I learned with you.

First, you need to know that there is no such thing as "junk food". There are two different things - food and junk. Junk may taste like food, but it is not. Do you know what the most consumed form of vegetables is in North America? It is ketchup, french fries and onion rings!

You are what you eat. You don't want to look like an onion ring, do you?

Be close to nature. Eat clean. This not only means washing your food well, but also embracing foods like vegetables, fruits and whole grains as well as healthy proteins and fats. Eating healthy is about eating more of the best and healthiest options in each of the food groups—and eating less of the not-so-healthy ones. It means cutting back on refined grains, added sugars, salt and unhealthy fats.

A refined grain is made by processing a natural, whole grain so that some or most of the nutrients are lost. Almost all grain products have been refined in one way or another.

White rice, pasta, cream of wheat, cookies, white bread and pastry are all examples of refined grain products.

Added sugars are sugars and syrups that are added to foods or beverages such as soft drinks, candy, ice cream and donuts when they are processed or prepared.

To make it easier to remember – try to eat less of three white things: sugar, salt and flour.

Drink water, lots of water.

Choose fresh food. Shop local. Go to farmers markets. Find places nearby where you can pick your own fruits and vegetables.

Consider buying free range, grass fed and organic produce. Remember if you eat chemicals, you become chemicals too.

These choices can get a bit costly, but I have found that eating quality food reduces the quantity I need. Healthy food fuels you better and you need less to keep your body and mind happy and healthy.

Educate yourself. Know what you are consuming. Read the label. And if you cannot pronounce ingredients or don't know them – do not eat them. Pay attention to the amount of sugar, sodium (salt) and saturated fats in foods. Nutrition facts are given per one serving only. Make sure that you know what one serving means. For example, on the box of crackers the label states "Per 4 crackers". This means if I had 10 crackers, I would need to multiply every line on the label 2.5 times to get the right numbers.

Read ingredients. How many ingredients do you think should be in a bottle of orange juice? One, maybe two items? Next time you go to the store, read the list of ingredients. You will be surprised.

There so many choices everywhere you go. The cheapest is not always the unhealthy one and the most expensive is not always the best option. Read, think, research and make good food choices.

You are what you eat. It is like putting gas into your car. The super clean gasoline costs more but your car will run on the same amount of fuel longer and stay cleaner. Some cars do not even run on regular gasoline. If you choose the cheaper fuel it will cost you more in repairs and it may even ruin your car.

Unlike cars, we cannot trade in a broken body as often as we want. Your body is the only one you were given. You will have it for the rest of your life. Give it the best fuel and make it last long and run well.

Chapter 21

Music and Laughter

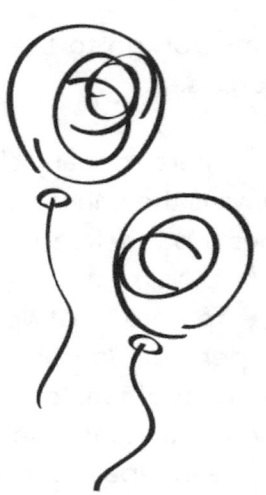

Do you play music?

Do you dance?

Do you listen to music?

How often do you laugh?

Do you know that one minute of laughter boosts your immune system for 24 hours?

There are a number of beneficial effects that music and laughter have on our bodies and minds, such as; reducing stress, easing pain, speeding up the recovery process, improving sleep quality, relieving symptoms of depression, improving cognitive performance, reducing anxiety and producing a general sense of well-being.

Find a radio station you enjoy, borrow some CDs from your public library, benefit from a summer performance of "Music in the

Park", take a dance class at your local community centre or watch your favourite comedy film.

Let yourself enjoy the music, and laugh! Smile!

Laughter will destroy anything negative.

Smile for at least two minutes a day. If you don't feel like smiling, hold a pen in your teeth. That will force your "smile" muscles to work and trick your brain into thinking that you are smiling.

Music and laughter - these are remedies you can access 24/7 and for free.

Be an artist. Paint your day. Find out who you are. Find your potential and your identity.

Remember that shadows always fall behind you when you face the sun.

Chapter 22

Happy Parents - Happy Kids

We all came to Canada for a better life. Most of us came here for a better life for our children.

We want our kids to be healthier and happier. We want them to have a better education, enhanced experiences and more rewarding careers. However, the one challenge parents face that they can never be ready for is – their kids! Children have their own ideas about their lives. Most of the time, they are not part of the decision to move to Canada and see this shift as a painful, unnecessary experience.

Immigrant children experience the same challenges as immigrant adults - difficulty learning a new language, adjusting to new systems and a new culture, finding friends, etc. The difference is that children's challenges are often underestimated or dismissed.

On top of the complexity that normal growth and development brings into any young person's life, immigrant children get an extra, uninvited bonus – separation from grandparents, extended family and friends. Without these built-in support systems, they can experience a lack of love, lack of harmony, lack of communication and an overall lack of control over their lives. These are all sensations that may shape their futures.

Immigration magnifies the natural generational differences in cultural values, knowledge and outlook. With immigration, the model of right and wrong often changes. It is only natural for children to wish to "fly", to seek out adventure and new experiences. They test the limits that their parents and others set and also test the consequences of taking risks. Under stressful conditions, children often resort to extreme measures, such as experimenting with drugs, running away from home or associating with groups that seek excitement in the wrong ways.

At the beginning, parents are preoccupied with their own problems of adjustment to new jobs, homes and social circumstances. They have pressures and priorities that often don't allow the time or place for meaningful family relationships or activities. Having already left so much behind, children can often feel deprived of parental attention too. They may feel isolated from people in general.

As time goes on, even though parents feel the need to do the best for their children, they may have difficulty following through. Children can reject their parents, considering them "out of touch". Parents may feel unable to influence their children and may withdraw to avoid conflict. Parents may also lack self-confidence in communicating with their children who adapt so quickly to the new environment. Adolescent and young adult children may appear more mature, competent, and opinionated than expected. They are often better educated, more open-minded and higher earning than their parents. All of these factors can create challenges in the parent-child relationship.

You must never lose faith in yourself and in your child's potential. Optimistic parental expectations are often an expression of your trust in yourself. Pessimistic expectations (reflecting distrust of yourself), can be projected onto your child.

Establish a working set of values, not necessarily "super-modern", but open-minded. You have the right to set specific values and expectations for your children; and you have the right to attempt to pass these values on. At the same time, you must respect your child's right to establish his or her own values.

Be honest with your children. Don't be afraid to admit your mistakes. Ask for an apology when you are "wrong". Don't just set limits; explain why you are setting them.

Remember, the stronger the bond, the more difficult it is for a child to break away. Talk to your kids. Be genuinely interested in their lives. Ask questions. Offer your opinion if asked. Listen.

Create a safe haven where you and your children can recuperate from the disappointments of the outside world. Put your arms around each other. Just be there.

Here is a list of questions to think about as you develop a strategy for building trusting relationships with your children:

- ✓ How much will I probe into my children's private lives?
- ✓ How much will I discuss my personal problems with them?
- ✓ How can I express my own viewpoint without becoming dogmatic?
- ✓ How much do I want to allow my children's participation in family decision-making?

- How much participation will I expect from them in family chores?
- Which activities will we do as a family and which ones should we do independently?
- How much should I structure my child's activities?
- How much guidance should I offer without being asked? When? How?
- When is it important to keep "hands off"?
- How do I plan to steer clear, without implying that I don't care?

I remember meeting a seven year old boy who was sent to Canada alone to study. He lived with a host family and had no family or friends around him. Can you imagine that little child alone in a strange country, speaking no English, and knowing nothing about anything?

I believe that his parents sent him here for the best. They invested a lot of money to support his development into a successful adult. But at what cost for the child? He was deprived of family, of a caring environment and, ultimately, of a normal childhood.

For him, the distance was real: his parents lived on another continent. You should know that your child may feel the same way, even though you are living under the same roof.

My friend shared a story that changed the way he interacts with his children and, in fact, changed his life.

One evening his son asked him how much money he makes. He looked at the child uncomfortably thinking that he was probably asking to buy a toy, and responded -"$30 per hour". His son asked if he could borrow $20 from him. The parent angrily reacted with a five minute tirade on how hard he works, how difficult it is to support the family, how tired he was, and then he sent his son to his room. A few minutes later he calmed down and knocked on the door of his son's room. He gave him $20 and asked what he needed it for. The child took the $20 and pulled another $10 out from under his pillow. Next he handed the $30 to his dad and asked if he could buy one hour of his time so that he could come home earlier tomorrow, have dinner with the family and play with him.

This event forced him to reevaluate his values and think about what was most important to him. From that day forward, he started spending more time with his children and subsequently learned a little of what the world looked like through his children's eyes.

There is no single formula on how to raise a child. There is no "how-to" manual or recipe book. However, I strongly believe this: to bring up healthy and happy children, you need to help them feel connected – to you, to extended family members, to friends, to neighbours and to their new community.

While we can't control our children's ultimate happiness, we can control our own. Parents, who are satisfied and happy, are a better influence on their own children. Children absorb everything from us. Our moods matter.

Happy parents are likely to have happy kids!

Here are some tips to help you avoid burnout and stay happy:

- ✓ Know your goal. Do you want to raise a happy and successful child? Yes, but first of all you are here to make sure they survive.

- ✓ Do not expect gratitude.
- ✓ Do not insist they do what you think are "interesting things". Kids will find what they are interested in on their own.
- ✓ Don't be afraid of failure.
- ✓ Find a mentor – someone you trust who will listen and tell you: "It's Ok to feel that way, you are just tired".

Chapter 23

STICK OR SPLIT

*E*very relationship has ups and downs which every couple learns to deal with. However, immigration challenges, adapting to a new culture, learning a new language and adopting new behaviours can challenge even the strongest relationship. The way people handle these challenges can either hurt or reinforce their bond.

Challenges can bring couples closer together as spouses look to each other for support and connection. They can also break relationships apart, if couples are not prepared or able to adjust.

Here some challenges that put pressure on families:

- Shifting roles and changing individual needs
- Feelings of loss of identity
- Uncertainty about the present and future
- Culture shift
- Career stress
- Financial worry
- Confusion expressed as anger at a partner
- Loss of self-esteem and self-worth
- Emotional and physical separation
- A new sense of freedom and opportunity

Whatever the challenges you may face, here are some strategies that you can use to re-establish your bond in your new culture.

- Be open and honest – do not repress your true feelings.
- Share your new experiences, the challenges they pose for you and how you plan to handle them. Ask for suggestions on how to overcome difficulties.
- Learn to listen.
- Talk about your emotional wounds, but stop complaining.
- Take responsibility for your part in the relationship.
- Have quality time together – just the two of you.
- Stick to one issue at a time when arguing.
- Choose the best time to talk to each other – ask if it is OK to talk now?
- Grow and change for the better as a person, and support the changes in your partner.
- Don't give up your old friends.
- Share your passions. Show your partner what you love, so that he or she can experience it as you do.
- Compliment your partner – it is a good reminder of your love.
- Address problems and misunderstandings when they arise.
- Work on solving conflicts together, rather than blaming each other.

As your lives change in your new world, you may also change as a couple. Being able to move flexibly with the events of your new life is vital for you as an individual and for your relationships.

Some people believe that good relationships just evolve naturally; but, like anything else worth doing in life, you need to work on them. You can't change others, but you can change yourself and your attitude towards your partner.

How do you keep fighting for your love? How do you keep motivated while dealing with new experiences and stresses?

-
-
-
-
-

Love is within YOU. Draw on your strengths. Let your happy family be a bridge to your successful future. Create the relationships you want by growing yourself, not by trying to change others. Live the relationships you strive for.

However, if you find that there is no joy left in your relationship and no hope for change, don't wait for your children to grow up. You may have to admit that it's time to split and move on with your life.

You always have a choice – stick or split.

Chapter 24

WORKPLACE CULTURE

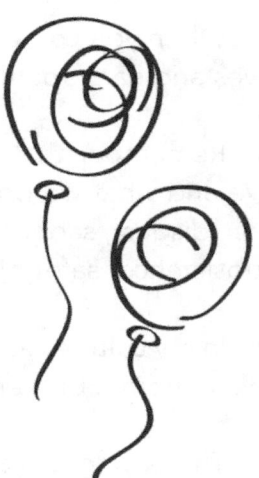

*H*ere are some general tips that are helpful to know about most Canadian workplace cultures:

- ✔ Be on time, meet deadlines.
- ✔ Work both independently and as a team member.
- ✔ Show initiative.
- ✔ Follow rules and procedures.
- ✔ Have a clear distinction between home life and work life.
- ✔ Express your opinion directly.
- ✔ Be open to differences.
- ✔ Ask questions.
- ✔ Make direct eye contact.
- ✔ Be aware of personal habits that might be distracting to others.
- ✔ Keep out of other people's personal space.

Observing the culture will help you fit in and find your place within it. While the tips listed above are common, all workplaces are different. Each workplace has its own culture, style, traditions and norms. Plus, people from all over the world are entering the workforce here and shaping Canadian workplaces in new ways.

When you come into a new workplace - look around; keep your eyes and ears open. Ask questions, be open and do not judge.

Remember that people are still people. No matter where we live and what we do, we still share the same emotions: happiness, fear, disgust, sadness, anger, etc. And we still have the same needs: subsistence, safety, importance, freedom, identity and justice.

In my culture we have a saying: "When visiting someone's place, feel at home, but remember that you are a guest".

This saying can also be applied to workplace culture – be yourself, but be considerate of others.

Chapter 25

SMALL TALK IS BIG TALK

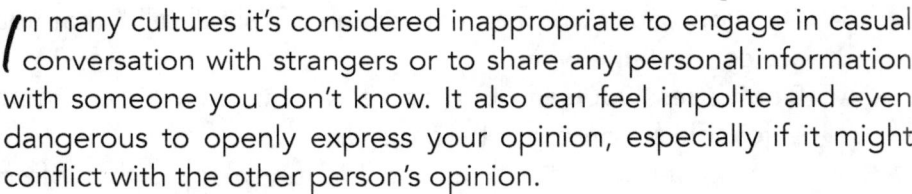

In many cultures it's considered inappropriate to engage in casual conversation with strangers or to share any personal information with someone you don't know. It also can feel impolite and even dangerous to openly express your opinion, especially if it might conflict with the other person's opinion.

Not so in Canada.

The role of "small talk" in Canadian culture is significant. It took me years to master this art. I am often surprised at how naturally and comfortably Canadians seem to do it. At first, when someone asked me - "how are things going?" or "how are you?" – I answered honestly and fully. I would tell them the details of my life and how my health was, my mood, etc. I naturally assumed that people were genuinely interested in the answer. Actually no one really paid attention to my response. In fact, I could see that they were often uncomfortable with the details of my answer, while I thought it would be rude to answer casually.

I eventually discovered that "How's it going?" and "How are you?" are just different ways of saying "Hello". They don't really require a long answer. By the way, the right answer is "Fine, and how are you?", followed by a minute or two of discussion about non-personal things such as the weather. After that, if you are still enjoying talking, the real conversation begins.

"Small Talk" is a critical tool in Canada for creating the first step of a personal bond. It is often used as a friendly opening to the main portion of the discussion, such as an interview or a meeting. You can be the most skilled worker, but your ability to build and maintain this initial relationship will be critical for your success.

Here are a few strategies to correctly incorporate "small talk" into your everyday life:

- Consider small talk as an opportunity for building successful relationships!
- Watch how others do it — the topics they cover, the tone they use, their style of verbal and non-verbal communication.
- Develop your own personal version of "small talk" that you are comfortable with.
- Don't stress yourself out. People who are relaxed are more enjoyable for others to be around.
- Plan something to talk about. Identify a topic that offers potential for common ground or share something interesting that's in the news. Make sure to avoid discussing politics, religion and sex. These are taboo topics for Canadian small talk.
- Start with a small compliment.
- Share something about yourself – anything, as long as it's not too personal.
- Most people love to talk about themselves, so ask questions that let them tell their best stories.
- Keep things light, fun and positive.
- Keep your ears open and see if something the person says will trigger a new line of conversation.
- Make people feel important by showing your interest in what they have to say. You can do this with eye contact, leaning

forward slightly, smiling and nodding and, of course, following up on his or her comments.

Most people won't remember what you did or what you said, but they will remember how you made them feel. Make people feel special!

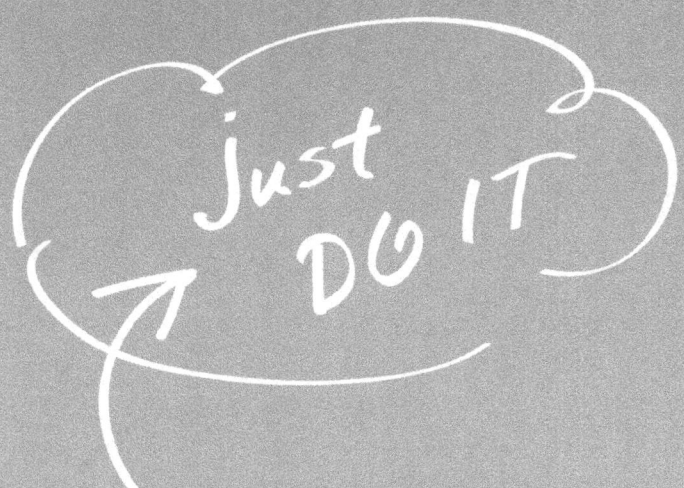

Only you can reach for the sky and stretch beyond it. Only you can break through the limits that hold you back.
Reach inside to find your strength; reach outside to find support; reach up, way up, to find your potential – and then, just do it!

"Stop counting crayons - just draw pictures".
Mark Scharenbroich

Chapter 26

HAVE A PLAN

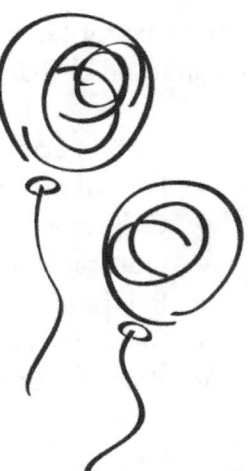

Do you know what the difference is between a dream and a goal? One word – action!

A dream acted upon has become a goal.

If you have a number of goals - list them.
List everything you want to achieve.
List everything you need to feel successful.

Your goal could be improving your English, getting a good job, bringing your family to Canada, buying a car, moving into your own home, feeling healthy and fit…

Make a list, and place it where you can see it often.
Then start working on your list by choosing one goal - the goal that you feel is the most essential for you to achieve right now.
Write down all the steps you have to take to reach this goal.
Make the list as detailed as possible.

For example, if you require a license to practice your profession in Canada, like I did, the list of steps might look like this:

- Get an application package from the regulatory body
- Fill out application forms
- Collect all necessary documents
- Get translations whenever required
- Pay fees
- Send in documents
- Prepare for the language test
- Find a school
- Get a library card
- Prepare for the professional exam
- Get experience in the field
- Get a volunteer placement
- Create a resume
- Prepare for an interview
- Meet people from the profession
- Find a mentor

You can make it even more detailed. For example, an action such as "Prepare for the language test" could be split to smaller steps:

- Learn about the test
- Find out what scores I need to pass
- Find preparation classes
- Attend classes
- Do homework
- Do more than just homework

The Sky is no Longer the Limit

Make a list and take action every day. Every day do something from your list that will get you closer to your dream.

Don't be discouraged when things don't always go the way you planned. Some things are outside your control. For example, you cannot push the regulatory body to assess your application faster; but you can continue working on your language skills and build your network while you wait.

List your goals here:

-
-
-
-
-

Write down one goal which would greatly impact you when achieved:

-

List actions you need to take to reach your goal:

-
-
-
-
-

Chapter 27

WORK ON YOUR PLAN

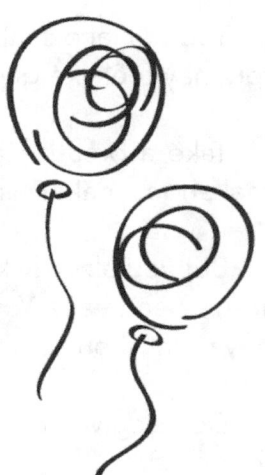

After you have created your initial list, start working on it. Start taking action today!

How many goals have never been achieved?
How many books have never been written?
How many millions of dollars have not been made?

Goals are only dreams if they are never acted upon.

You know what you want. You know how to get there.
You just need to start.
Start today.
Every day accomplish something from your list.

Review your plan often. Add new things. Check off the ones you have completed. Every day ask yourself: "What have I done today to make my dream become a reality?"

You don't have to accomplish big things every day.
Everything counts, as long as you move towards your goal.

You will face challenges - probably many challenges. Some days you may feel like giving up.

Take a breath. Take a deep breath and remember that facing challenges makes us stronger.

But you already know that. You are in Canada, and coming here hasn't been easy. You were strong enough to get here. Carry on by staying and pursuing what you came here for.

Do not give up. Take a pause. Recuperate - and move on toward your dream.

Thomas A. Edison said: "Our greatest weakness lies in giving up. The most certain way to succeed is always to try just one more time".

Work hard and celebrate your successes along the way.

Think about something you enjoy.
Promise to treat yourself with it when you reach a certain objective.

I remember preparing for a professional exam. I had four months to prepare. Every free minute, night and day, I was studying. I was reading, writing, memorizing and grasping everything I could. Sometimes I was tempted to do anything but study; however, I kept my eyes on my goal and on the reward I promised myself.

After taking the exam, I claimed my reward. Do you know what I promised myself?

I allowed myself to read one book in my own language: one book, one short book that I swallowed in a day. And then I started working on achieving my next goal.

One step at a time. One step, one small step. Every day.

Chapter 28

DEVELOP GOOD HABITS

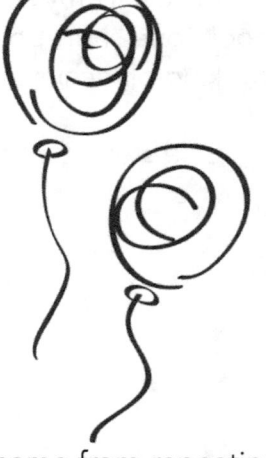

We all find comfort in our routines. Habits come from repeating the same tasks, timelines and decisions over and over again. What we did yesterday, we will do today, whether this is right for us or wrong. Our habits define who we are and how others judge our character.

Routine allows us to handle the everyday challenges we face in life. Habits are not necessarily bad, but they often develop because we haven't created an alternative. We automatically follow the action plan our brains have been programmed to tell us, instead of doing what we have actually planned in the first place.

Have you ever realized that following a habit defers responsibility for your actions?

In the workplace, our habits have a significant impact on how productive we are and on how our colleagues perceive us.

We all have bad habits, but habits don't just happen without our "input". We develop good and bad habits over time. The good news is we can change them! Having a better understanding of your bad habits will help you develop the good ones you really want in your life.

Habits can influence the success of your career.

Here are just a few that can cost you your job: procrastination, social media addiction, gossiping, complaining, arriving late or returning late from breaks, not responding to e-mails, always wanting to do things on your own and speaking without thinking first. Do you see yourself in any of these?

Take a look at yourself, and (be brave), ask others about your habits too.

Once you understand and acknowledge your bad habits, you can change them for good habits that will help you advance in your career and be more fulfilled in your personal life.

We all give ourselves excuses of why "now" is not the right time to create new habits– "I'm too busy", "I'm too tired" "The kids are starting school". Determine the specific element of the process that is holding you back and plan a solution for yourself that works within your life structure. Turn your project into a game - with you as the winner! Getting rid of bad habits will give you the energy to do the things that really matter.

Change may take time and push you out of your comfort zone. The most important part of building a new habit is staying consistent. It doesn't matter how well you perform on any individual day. Constant effort and keeping your eye on the goal is what makes the real difference. When you start a new habit, take it slowly. Remember that baby steps are still steps in the right direction.

When you make a mistake, focus on developing a plan to get back on track as quickly as possible. Don't spend your energy blaming yourself or feeling guilty – move on and go back to working on yourself.

Keep a record of your changes. Write them down regularly no matter how small they are. It's important to keep a record of positive changes and completed tasks, because the more things you put there, the better you feel about yourself. Be proud of what you have achieved. Share your accomplishments with others. We all feel good when our achievements are recognized.

Chapter 29

THE POWER OF ASKING

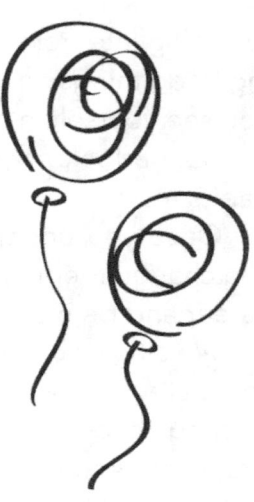

NO

I said, NO!

How many No's do you need before you stop asking? One, two, ten…?

Or maybe you don't even take the chance.

Do you think about what you need to ask and then decide "THIS IS STUPID!" -and so you never ask!

When it comes to asking, think about children!
How many times a day do they ask if they want or need something?

One, two, one hundred…? Children will ask as many times as it takes to get a "Yes." When they hear "No", the game has just started!

For example, my son has a sweet tooth. His day usually starts with "I want something sweet" and he keeps asking, begging, crying, and negotiating until he gets the sweets or gets a very firm "No." These conversations happen every day, a few times a day. But he never gives up. When he wants something, he just keeps on asking.

Have you heard about the "Law of attraction"? There are a number of books, workshops, and videos on this phenomenon. In short, the law of attraction can be described as "like attracts like". Basically, it states that a person, by focusing on positive or negative thoughts, brings positive or negative experiences into his or her life.

If you want to attract something into your life, do the following:

First, vocalize exactly what you want. Say it out loud.
Second, imagine in detail what your dream looks like.
Third, imagine that you already have it.

My son is not familiar with the theory of the law of attraction. He has not read any books, watched any videos, or attended classes on this topic. But he knows exactly HOW to ask for what he WANTS!

I remember one time he saw a cartoon character skating on a skate board.
From that moment, he started dreaming about a skate board.
He drew a picture of his skate board and placed it on a cork board in his room. He used anything - a pillow, a book, a newsletter - to help envision himself skate-boarding.

Plus, he constantly asked us to buy him one.

I had a clear idea of what he wanted and I knew how much money I wanted to spend.

One day I went to the store and saw a red skate board for $100.00.

My son wanted blue one, and I was prepared to spend only half of that price. I safely made it out of that store. In the next two minutes, I found a blue skate board at a 60 percent discount and my son achieved his goal. That is how the law of attraction works.

But you don't always have to pay for it with money.

If you think positively about what you want, if you smile and enjoy seeing others achieve their dreams, if you picture yourself in the moment – you will attract everything you want. Notice what you pay attention to when you are looking at magazines. Do you notice things you like or things you dislike? Remember - to change what you get in life, you need to change what you focus on!

Attraction is also love. Give love, joy, positivity, gratitude, passion…and you will get back what you give!

What types of people are you most likely to help? People who ask for help, or those who do not?

Don't be afraid to ask. Ask for feedback, ask for directions in your life, ask for information, ask for referrals and ask for help. You won't lose anything by asking. The worst that can happen is that you get "No" for an answer (leaving you with the same result you would get if you didn't ask).

Use your internal guidance system to determine when, what and how to ask.

Never let an undeserving or shameful feeling stop you from asking!

Chapter 30

CHOOSE YOUR EMPLOYER

*H*ow many jobs have you had in your life?

How many do you need right now?

You need only one good job! So choose your employer wisely.

Work takes up a huge part of your life and affects all areas of your being.
It could contribute to your happiness or steal it away.
It could enhance your skills or destroy your self-esteem.
Your choice of employer can make a big difference. Employers come in all sorts of shapes and sizes and they offer a diverse range of working environments, training options and opportunities for career development.

What are the key things you would want to see from your ideal employer?

- ✓ Size
- ✓ Company culture
- ✓ Location
- ✓ Work/life balance

- ✓ Training
- ✓ Career paths
- ✓ Travel

Make a list:

- ✓
- ✓
- ✓
- ✓
- ✓
- ✓
- ✓

You can find out about these things by researching on the internet; by talking to people in the industry or people who already work for an employer you are interested in; or by asking questions during the face-to-face interview.

Your choice of company will help steer your career in the right direction. Know where you want to go; and then analyze how this job and this employer could help you reach your personal goals and provide opportunities for professional growth. Look around at other opportunities before making a decision.

Consider working for yourself! There are plenty of resources and organizations that will help you if you're interested in starting your own business.

Whether you work for someone or you have your own business, give your best to everything you do. Be passionate about what you do. Use your personal skills to enhance the service or the product you are working on. When you find a job that fits your needs and expectations, results will come much more naturally.

Chapter 31

MARKET YOURSELF

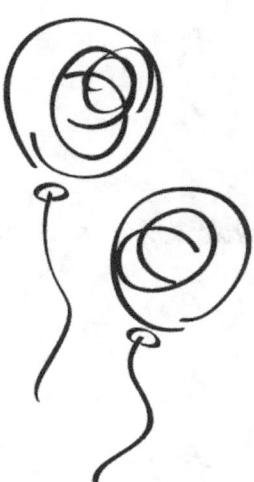

Marketing yourself is a way to demonstrate why someone would want to hire you. You might be afraid to market yourself, but that is what searching for a job is all about. You create your own luck and it starts with marketing the best product you have - You!

Know your value. Analyze your weaknesses and see whether you can show them as strengths. For example, an accent could be a stumbling block or a charming identifier. It might mean a communication challenge or a communication advantage, since it means you speak more than one language and have international experience.

We all have a unique set of gifts, experiences, accomplishments, ideas and interests that make us stand out. Identify yours and communicate them to the world!

Write down what you want from a job:

⌣

⌣

⌣

-
-

Write down what you have to offer an employer:

-
-
-
-
-

Identify three reasons that answer the question "Why hire me?"

-
-
-

The real purpose of your resume is to get you interviews. Make it visible! Consider that your resume has less than one minute to spark interest. Most employers are looking for candidates who closely match the skills and experience they are seeking. So market the skills and abilities employers want to see.

Create a strategy for getting interviews. Consider the following:

- ✓ Tell everyone that you're looking for a job.
- ✓ Join a job search group.
- ✓ Post your resume on the Job search sites.
- ✓ Call people and companies you want to work for.
- ✓ Ask for informational interviews.
- ✓ Ask if someone is hiring.
- ✓ Direct your networking by seeking out specific people.
- ✓ Make your job hunt a daily routine.
- ✓ Keep your eyes and ears open.

Work on your resume and cover letter. Build your network and LinkedIn profile. Use these tools to describe your particular uniqueness: market yourself as the best person for the position.

When preparing for a job interview, it is important to believe in your skills and abilities. Confidence is the key to effectively presenting yourself. Develop the right job interview mindset, focused on your strengths. Think about what makes you unique. Impress the interviewer with your knowledge of the company. Ask questions that show you've done your research. Demonstrate how you can help move the company forward.

After the interview, send a note of thanks highlighting your skills and reminding the interviewer "why hire me".

Create your image; create your outlook. Build on your strengths and weaknesses. Believe in yourself and remember that you need just one job. One good job!

Chapter 32

EDUCATE YOURSELF

Most people don't educate themselves after graduating from school and the results speak for themselves: they don't achieve the success they want.

I believe that many human beings are "hard-wired" to be poor and unhappy.

This "wiring" creates a simple action plan - acquire and consume. On top of this natural wiring, we also have our early childhood programming from parents and friends – much of which was negative.

Think about how different your life would be if you had received more positive programming. The path to success is not always obvious; in fact, it is actually the opposite of our natural inclinations.

You have the opportunity to learn every day of your life. Take advantage of the opportunity!

You can take a class, read a book, browse the web for interesting articles and talk to people around you.

The world changes every day. It's important to keep up with what's happening in the world, so that life won't pass you by.

The more you learn, the more you see. The more you know, the more you want to know. Lifelong learning is a fitness club for your brain. It brings you to a whole new level of enlightenment. Lifelong learning puts your life in perspective, helps you to understand the world around you better and brings greater meaning to your life.

You may not change your mind on some subjects, but you will appreciate that there is always more than one side to every problem.
Devoting yourself to lifelong learning can break through the barriers to your success.
Keeping current in your field is essential to your professional life. Expand your mind and learn something new every day. Learn from your personal experiences, your successes and your failures. Fear is one of the barriers that can prevent you from becoming what you really want to be. Fear often comes from the unknown and the best way to fight the unknown is to learn.
Invest in your future, because that is where you are going to spend the rest of your life.

Chapter 33

DO YOU SPEAK ENGLISH?

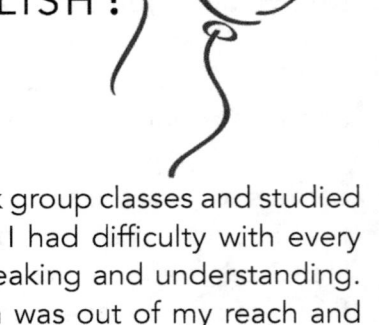

I tried to learn English back home. I took group classes and studied with a private tutor. Nothing worked. I had difficulty with every aspect of English – reading, writing, speaking and understanding. After a few trials, I thought that English was out of my reach and that I would never speak it - ever!

And then we moved to Canada. Here I thought speaking English would just come naturally. After all, I lived in an English speaking environment; I went to English stores and watched English language TV! Two months later, nothing had changed. I simply did not absorb the language as I had hoped.

The money we brought from home was disappearing fast so we started immediately looking for jobs. Checking out my neighborhood, I found that every job required English. The only alternative was to work within my own cultural community. For me, this was not an option. I wanted to learn the language. There are too many examples of immigrants failing to learn or improve their English because they work within their own language environment. Some may live in Canada for 20 years and still never learn to communicate in English (or French if they landed in Quebec).

I wanted to be successful…I had no choice but to set my mind on conquering the language. I had to find a way!

I used various techniques to improve my English. Some of these may also work for you:

- Listen a lot to people speaking English around you, listen to English TV and radio, listen to everything.
- Learn the meaning of unfamiliar words, then write them down and use them.
- Concentrate on the language content that is relevant to you.
- Really focus on what you understand.
- Train your speech muscles by using them often.
- Use English as a tool to communicate at every opportunity.
- Start using new words and then phrases.
- Focus on the core (about 1,000 words).
- Practice!
- Find a conversation buddy.
- Find someone you feel comfortable with and ask them to correct you.
- Record your pronunciation in a way that works for you. Then listen to the recording and correct yourself.
- Take a deep breath and relax.
- Allow yourself to make mistakes!

Most people who speak only one language would love to speak more than one. They are fascinated by your bravery in coming to Canada and learning a foreign language. Talk to people. Express yourself in English, and stop apologizing for your language!

Chapter 34

KNOW YOUR RIGHTS

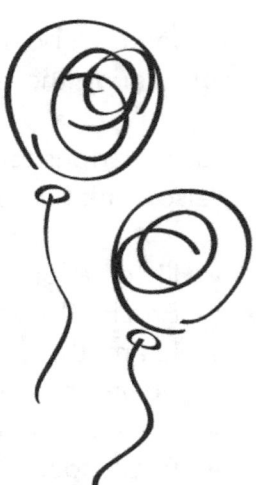

In Canada you enjoy many rights in every area of your life: in public places, at work, at school, at home, in health-care facilities, etc.

In order to exercise your rights, you need to know them. Educate yourself. Observe, read, and ask questions.

Ask for what you need and want; try to have as much input as possible in making your own life decisions.

For example, when you are a patient, you have the right to:

- ask questions about and understanding your medical care;
- get a second opinion if you wish to seek one;
- make an informed decision;
- ask about your health care provider's experience and credentials;
- express your concerns about quality of care and to take action if it is inadequate; and
- refuse care or medical treatment if you choose.

When you have a medical condition, you have a right to be accommodated at your workplace. For example, if you have diabetes, you can request regular work breaks to manage your condition.

You have the right to be treated equally. "Equal" does not necessarily mean "the same", but it does mean that everyone has an equal opportunity to participate.

You may not always know if your rights are being disrespected, but I would encourage you to speak up when:

- you feel something is not right;
- you have been poorly treated;
- you need to correct misinformation or assumptions;
- you have a complaint;
- you want to be heard; or
- you need something.

Although I found it difficult to speak up for myself, I had no difficulty speaking up for others – my family, friends, colleagues or strangers. I would readily raise my voice to support someone in need or someone being treated unfairly. It took some courage at first, but it got easier through practice.

By letting others know how you feel about issues that affect your life, you can help make changes to the way you are treated or how something is done. At the same time, you are educating others.

I remember being very upset by a call centre representative's attitude. I told the person that the way she spoke to me made me cry. She was definitely taken aback by my comment and apologized. She also provided me with all the information she originally withheld. And I hope, after this incident, that she will be more considerate when talking to others.

As a parent, you must protect your children's rights as well. Advocate for your kids. Listen attentively to their conversations, ask questions, trust them and do not excuse the inappropriate behaviour of others.

When your children start at a new school, ask for a tour. Visit the school together with your child prior to the first day of school and ask to have your child buddied up with someone of the same age. Make sure that you and your child know the school rules and have the names of people to ask for help when needed. Build a relationship with the teacher and check on your child's progress or any problems that need to be addressed. Participate in school life by volunteering at events, school tours or the parent's council.

In Canada, you have rights - do not let others take them away from you.

Know your rights and use them, but don't forget that you have obligations too.

When you immigrate to Canada, you have an obligation to follow the laws and regulations of the country, to be a positive, contributing member of society and to strive for citizenship. As a citizen, you have both the right and an obligation to vote and to support the country's legal system by serving on a jury if called to do so.

Chapter 35

Find a Mentor

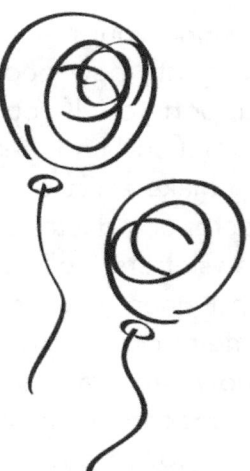

People are gifts. Some of them have gone through the experiences you are going through now. Find good people who know the art of being successful. There are lots of generous people and they want to help you. Find these people; tell your story and share some of your plans. Talk to people, listen to their stories and pursue further meetings with those you can learn from.

There are several networking programs that will help you find people who can open up new horizons for you. People who participate in these programs find many ways to help each other. Grab these networking opportunities with passion - these people may be responsible for many positive changes in your life. Listen to their ideas, act upon what makes sense and show them your results.

Keep in mind that a person who offers his time in return for compensation is not the same thing as a mentor. Advisers and consultants can be very helpful; however, true mentors are effective because they are only interested in helping you succeed.

Think about how open, flexible, thoughtful and approachable you are. Are you somebody you would like to mentor? Are you eager to learn and committed to change and growth? Become the person that others would love to support and nurture.

Find your mentors among the people you know, but also connect with new people who will find it a beneficial experience to support you. If you don't know any inspiring people, you need to go out and find them.

Make a list of successful people in your community. Look for sector or industry-specific events and groups. Subscribe to relevant newsletters. Follow interesting individuals on Twitter or LinkedIn. And when you are ready, get in touch and ask for 30 minutes of time to chat. Do not be afraid to send emails to people you do not know personally.

Prepare what you want to ask. Explain what excites you about your goal, be honest about your fears and ask for feedback. It is rarely a good idea to make a formal request like "Will you be my mentor?" This relationship takes time to grow. Start by asking for advice on one project or problem, and move on from there.

Ask for feedback and take time to reflect on it. Try not to explain yourself or your actions, just listen and learn. Make sure you understand what is being said and why. Ask for clarification if you are not sure. Learn from each suggestion and focus on how to improve.

Usually, the opinions that matter are from those who know that you could do better and make it a point to tell you.

It's important to nurture the mentoring relationship. Thank your mentor and show how much s/he has helped you.

People are presents that you need to embrace and value.

If you struggle to find a mentor, remember that the answers to all your questions are right inside of you! Just believe in your potential - you have much more to offer than you realize. Imagine yourself in the shoes of those you deeply value and respect. Then imagine yourself already achieving this great success. Ask your future self what to do. And go for it!

Chapter 36

EXPLORE AND FEEL AT HOME

When you make a new start by moving to another country, province, city or neighborhood, it's only natural to experience challenges and discomfort, which may interfere with your journey to success. In so many little (and big) ways, you will compare your own culture to new ways of living in Canada. You will find some things different and other things weird. Your best approach is to keep an open mind to the differences. Try not judge. Remember that your culture is only one of many. Before you know it, your own concepts of the right way and the wrong way of doing things will start to shift.

I remember being surprised to see people eating and drinking on the go; or women putting on makeup or doing their hair in public places. This was very different from what I was used to and it was difficult not to judge them. But now I carry around my bottle of water, tea mug and snacks. Now I consider this normal, convenient and healthy.

Look for similarities to your culture. They will give you comfort. Notice differences and seek to understand and embrace Canadian culture. Merge the two in rich diversity and realize the beauty of Canada!

Explore your new neighbourhood, your city, your province and your new country! Find your favourite places- a library, a café, a restaurant, an apple farm, a beach, a park bench, a street, a museum, a conservation park, a campsite – and return to them regularly.

Meet and talk to people, try new foods, ask questions and don't be afraid to get out of your comfort zone and be silly. Create positive memories, write them down and send them to your friends so they too can share your experiences.

Keep your own cultural and family traditions, but also explore new traditions and adopt the ones you like.

Some of my favourite adopted traditions are: celebrating Thanksgiving in Algonquin Park by enjoying a lunch at the visitor's centre, while looking at the changing colours; celebrating Canada Day at Pelee Island with both the locals and visitors; listening to live music at one of the older wineries in Canada; and greeting new neighbours with homemade bread and a "welcome to the neighbourhood" card.

You can feel at home anywhere – in a hotel room, at a cottage, or living in a different country – as long as you appreciate it.

Chapter 37

YOU ARE UNIQUE

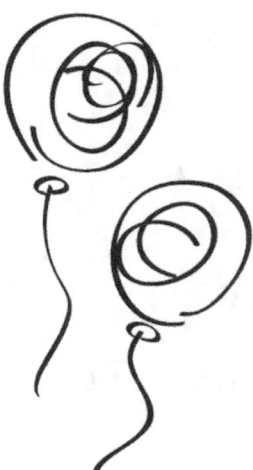

Congratulations! You have reached the last chapter of this book.

You now know that you and your path to success in Canada are unique.

Always be aware of what is happening to you and around you.

Live your life to the fullest.

Love what you do and what surrounds you. Canada offers so many experiences to enjoy: nature, people, cultures, places, seasons, activities and so much more.

Work hard and play hard. Balance your life.

Set ambitious goals and reach them!

You are the creator of your own life, START NOW and write the next chapter of this book – the next chapter of your life - your happy and successful life in Canada!

Chapter 38

WRITE THE NEXT CHAPTER OF THIS BOOK

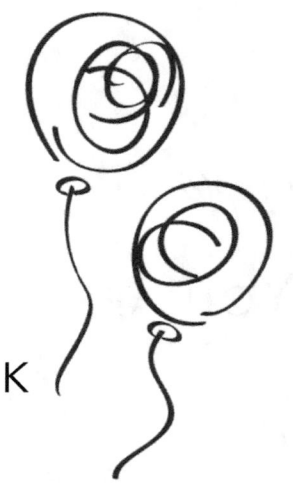

This chapter is to help you visualize the future you want so you can look at what you need to do to get there.

Let's first take a look where you are now:

What does my family life look like now?

-
-
-

What does my home look like?

⌣

⌣

⌣

What does my professional life look like now?

⌣

⌣

⌣

What am I thankful for at this moment?

⌣

⌣

⌣

In Seven Years….

My Family life is …..

)

)

)

My Home looks like…

)

)

)

My Career is…

)

)

)

The Sky is no Longer the Limit

Seven years from today will be _____day _____ months _____year.

Today is one of my usual days. I wake up around _____ a.m. I live in _____

and I am happy here because _____
_____.

I am _____ years old and I feel _____
_____.

I look at my reflection in the mirror and I see _____
_____.

My favourite activities are _____
_____.

My favourite people I love to spend time with are _____
_____.

My next vacation I will spend in _____
_____.

Today was a good day because _____
_____.

Tomorrow will be even better because _____
_____.

My plans for this year are _____
_____.

I have created my life – and I love what I have created!

Today's date _____

Signature _____

Remember that the key to your success is inside of you! Just believe in your own potential. You have much more to offer than you realize.

Imagine yourself in the shoes of those you deeply value and respect. Then imagine yourself achieving this great success. Ask your future self what to do in various situations –and then act on it!

When I was a child, I looked to the horizon and wondered what was on the other side of it. Somehow, in spite of all life's limitations, I believed my world would stretch beyond that line which always seemed just out of reach.

And so, I flew to Canada.

In a 747, we surged past the horizon and beyond, to the other side of the world.

And that flight was only the beginning. After seven years in Canada, I have demonstrated with my life what I always knew in my bones: we can draw our own horizons.

The Sky is no longer the limit, because it never really was!

www.ingramcontent.com/pod-product-compliance
Lightning Source LLC
LaVergne TN
LVHW051605070426
835507LV00021B/2770